UP

the

IVY

Ladder

UP
the
IVY
Ladder

Norman Runnion

Doubleday & Company, Inc.,
Garden City, New York
1969

Library of Congress Catalog Card Number 69–20095
Copyright © 1969 by Norman Runnion
All Rights Reserved
Printed in the United States of America
First Edition

To Marge

CONTENTS

24137

*Do About Pot . . . If Only Beer Didn't Come in Cans
. . . How to Avoid Charges of Administration Brutality.*

INTRODUCTION

This is a book of instructions on how to become a college president. It has been written to fill a void. There are books on how to repair cars, paint houses and tour Europe on an inadequate amount of dollars per day. Admittedly it is important to know how to do these things. But it is hard to conceive that a mastery of their techniques will be of vast benefit to American society.

The same cannot be said of learning how to become a college president. This is one of the most critical occupations in the country. If mass education is going to help solve many of our ills, then it is vital that our colleges and universities be directed by men and women of integrity, imagination and talent.

Reading and studying this book will not give anyone integrity, imagination and talent. Those characteristics must be acquired through heredity and environment, and are beyond the author's humble powers of creation. But for a person who has them, the author is hoping to point the way toward a career in which they can be brought to full flower.

Lest anyone be discouraged, it must also be pointed out that there are college presidents who are unimaginative, untalented and lacking in integrity. If the reader is in this category, he can still benefit from this guidebook. The job pays fairly well and brings with it a great deal of prestige. This should be sufficient motivation for any person wishing to make a place for himself in the world, regardless of his moral or mental qualities.

One objective of this book is to strip away some of the frightening myths that surround the position of college president. Too often, the public image of the president has been that of an austere figure in a flowing academic gown, surrounded by books of difficult philosophy. The thought of having to read all those books has deterred many young men and women from taking up this particular career.

Yet the reality of the situation is that a college president need not, and sometimes should not, be an academic expert. The reader will find, therefore, that the emphasis here is on common sense rather than library research. This means that the study involved in becoming a college president is relatively easy and allows plenty of time for golf and bridge.

The book assumes that anyone who follows its instructions can become a college president. The chances of success are higher if the reader is a young man or woman in high school or the early years of college who can mold his or her career from the beginning. However, middle-aged persons who have a yen to do something constructive in their retirement could start in the admissions office and move up from there.

Hopefully, the person who will benefit most from the advice is the potential student revolutionary. The author believes that more can be accomplished for the good of mankind by working from inside the Establishment than by trying to smack it down from the outside. It also is less painful this way, since those on the inside do not get tear-gassed.

The youngster interested in reforming society can choose no more rewarding line of work than that of a college president. Years ago, the function of the president was to run an institution that catered only to mankind's intellectual elite. The Affluent Society and the American Dream changed this. A college education has become a requirement for a job—almost any job—rather than a purely intellectual achievement.

Furthermore, the growth of state colleges and universities, coupled with the increased availability of federal and private scholarship money, has put this college education within the financial reach of almost anyone. A bachelor's degree now has roughly the same significance that a high school diploma had thirty years ago.

This has meant a change in the role of the college president. No longer can his institution be an exclusive center for quiet study and scholarship. Now he has to provide the mass education that once was the exclusive province of the high school principal.

His being charged with this responsibility makes the college president a major force, for good or possibly evil, in contemporary society. The job is worth having, particularly when colleges are being founded as fast as they are throughout the world. Openings always are available for candidates who have mastered the lessons of this book.

1

THE APPRENTICESHIP:
Where to Find the Ivy

Let it be clear from the start that there is one painless method of becoming a college president. If you are sufficiently famous, you can start at the top, omitting such nominal prerequisites as deanships and faculty meetings. Dwight D. Eisenhower, for one, did this at Columbia University before moving on to the White House. However, his previous experience included commanding armies locked in combat, and this was a good substitute for deanships.

Unfortunately it can take years to become famous, unless you are a student revolutionary who appears consistently on television. If you are an active revolutionary, you stand an odds-on chance of occupying the office of college president. But you will have to serve without pay. Also the occupation will be temporary, thus depriving you of many of the long-term joys of being a college president. These include sending your children to college free of charge and retiring as an emeritus knowing that you have done your best to rectify mankind's ills.

In any case, education in the United States today is far too important and complex to be left in the hands of academic amateurs and student revolutionaries. The times call for greatness in the presidential office. The great college presidents are those who thoroughly understand the nature of campus life.

It can be argued that one trouble with higher education today is that too few presidents have the capacity for this understanding. Many have gone into the presidential office directly from years of loyal service on the faculty. A lifetime as a professor has given them a one-sided view of educational responsibilities. It has made them wary of students, leary of public relations, and ignorant of fund-raising.

Still others have become presidents after long and successful careers as fund-raisers. This has caused them to regard students merely as sources of tuition revenue, and professors as scandalous spenders. Their work has kept them out of touch with the day-to-day intellectual encounters that are vital to the academic atmosphere of a great college.

Advantages of a Middle Course

This book of instructions, then, aims at a middle course which will provide you with the well-rounded background necessary to deal with all phases of the academic world. It would be possible for you to become a college president by following either of the paths mentioned above. Yet you would be lacking in what are surely the proper qualifications for the job.

Another advantage of the course of action proposed herein is that it is more varied and consequently more stimulating. Years spent only as a professor or as a fund-raiser can lead either to mental stagnation or else a warped view of human nature. You might consider all humanity either as students incapable of understanding your lectures or as tightwads who won't give you any money.

These parochial outlooks, which would adversely affect your chances of being a great college president, will be avoided by following the route up the academic ladder outlined in these pages. To begin with, you should follow your formal education with a year or two of teaching. This is extremely important. The months you spend in a classroom, lecturing to students and grading their papers, will help form the authoritarian complex that is necessary to get things done as a president.

Then you should become an administrator. Before you are fully trained, you should acquire the expertise involved in being a dean of students, an academic dean, the director of admissions, the director of public relations, and the director of development. These jobs will provide you with a panoramic view of campus activity.

How to Impress Trustees as Well as Faculty

In the end, the question of whether you will reach the top will depend largely on how the board of trustees judges your performance in these various administrative departments. You can see, therefore, that you need not overextend yourself in your undergraduate years trying to get a reputation as a scholar. You need only work hard enough on grades to be able to slip into graduate school. It would be a waste of time to become known to the trustees as a man more familiar with Beowulf than with a budget.

The point is that you always will be able to hire someone to teach Beowulf, at a lower salary than the one you will get as president. But you may have to pay out a lot of money for an accountant who will be able to give the budget the careful scrutiny it deserves. This is because a college or a university is primarily a business concern. In the case of Harvard or the University of California, it is a corporation of the complexity of General Motors or the United States Government. A pure academic could no more run one of these universities than a political scientist with a Ph.D. in political theory could get Congress to do his bidding.

Even within a college, a purely scholarly background can be a handicap. As soon as you become a president known for your profound thesis on the irrelevance of Einstein's relativity, a bright young professor will come along and tell his colleagues that you are an idiot. This will hurt both your feelings and your image.

Similarly, you must be careful when you choose your field of study. If you are a physicist, you will be accused by the chemists of favoring the physicists at their expense. The physicists will be angry because they will claim that you are leaning over backwards to let the chemists buy new equipment.

The humanists will dislike you just because you are a scientist.

The reverse will be true if you are of the humanities.

This considerably narrows your potential fields of study, but it does leave you with carpentry and the social sciences. In the end, no matter who you are or what you have studied, you will be distrusted by all or part of the faculty when you become president. This is because they know in their own hearts that you are not as smart as they are. However, if you combine your Ph.D. with acute business sense, you will be respected. Good businessmen know how to make money. If there is anything a faculty member likes, it is money. Money buys equipment and books and pays for salaries and sabbaticals, and to hell with Beowulf.

The Necessity of Having a Ph.D.

The trouble with carpentry is that you might have difficulty getting a Ph.D. in this field. Without a Ph.D., you will suffer. You can spend two years in nursery school, eight years in grade school, four years in high school, four years in college, one year in graduate school acquiring a master's degree, and two years studying for a Ph.D. Up until the last two years, you are a dolt. It is only when you receive your Ph.D. and have those magical letters "Dr." affixed to your name that your academic colleagues will allow you the distinction of being called an educated man.

To explore this further, let us consider what could be the reaction of a typical college president. The door to his office bursts open and a student rushes in.

"Guess what, Sir," the student says. "My uncle is retiring, and he told me he would be willing to come here and be a professor. At last, we will have someone who can teach us something!"

"And what, may I ask, does your uncle do?" the president inquires.

"He started out as an alderman, was elected a state representative, then became a Congressman, got elected to the Senate for three consecutive terms, was appointed to the Cabinet as Postmaster General, and has just served successfully as campaign manager for the President in the last election. He wants to teach 'Political Practice.'"

"Where did he get his Ph.D.?"

"He didn't. He just has a bachelor's."

"I'm sorry," the president says. "It wouldn't look good in the catalogue. Besides, I can't believe that he is qualified as a scholar."

Suppose that at this point you come to the college for an appointment with the president to be considered as the new political practice instructor. Clutched in one hand is a Xerox copy of your newly won Ph.D. In the other is a bound volume of your doctoral thesis, "Statistical Relationships Between the Number of Stamps Sold and Political Activity in the United States Postmaster General's Office— A Case Study."

"That's very impressive," the president says. "I would like to read it one day. I think you will make an excellent addition to our staff."

The point about the thesis is that no one has studied this particular relationship before, which has made it an ideal subject for a doctoral dissertation. It will have contributed in its small way to the total sum of knowledge available on the planet, and this is a requirement for a Ph.D. thesis. It also will have made you an expert on one particular segment of this total knowledge, and that, too, is a purpose of the Ph.D.

Furthermore, the thesis was done in the field of political science, and that is good practical background for your career as a college president. A knowledge of politics is an essential element of academic administration, since professors and students engage in this activity constantly. You will be helped immensely in your constant struggles to stay ahead of the game if you know more about politics than do your opponents.

You must also remember that a college presidency can be the launching pad to future political glory. Always keep in mind that Woodrow Wilson went to the White House after being president of Princeton.

The Ideal Place to Start

The ideal place to start on your academic career is at a small, and preferably new, liberal arts college. These are not totally stifled by tradition, as is the case with universities and older colleges. The young institutions often permit more freedom of thought and action. The people who count will notice you more quickly, whereas in a place like Princeton you may be so insignificant that you will be ignored. Remember that one secret of any successful career is being noticed. It is not so much a matter of apple polishing as it is of finding someone to accept the apple.

Perhaps you will have read that small liberal arts colleges are on their last legs. You may be afraid lest you be associated with a loser. True, academic morticians are saying that the small liberal arts institutions are in danger of being killed off by powerful high schools and the multiversities. It is safe for you to ignore these predictions.

Always bear in mind that there is a primary principle of higher education: wherever a teenager exists, a director of admissions is ready to grab him. Otherwise colleges would not be able to meet their budgetary requirements. From the law of supply and demand, you can safely deduce that small liberal arts colleges, if properly administered, will continue to be around far into the future. Either that, or the multiversities will become so large that they will have to be admitted separately into the union, each with its own state flag.

An advantage of the newer schools is that you will not find it difficult to get a job with one. Their standards are lower than those of the universities. Academic openings are listed in trade journals, or made available at scholarly meetings. If you enjoy travel, pick an area such as New England which has a small, and often new, liberal arts college in almost any village. Then simply get in your car and drive from one college to another until someone hires you.

You may be particularly lucky just before the start of school in September. Perhaps a professor of political science has returned from a long, relaxing summer vacation and concluded that he simply could not face another year of dealing with students. He has therefore resigned, creating an opening for the first person to come along.

Perhaps, also, the admissions department has caught more freshmen in its dragnet than it had expected. This increased tuition revenue will make the president happy. But the academic dean will insist that another professor be hired to handle the crowd. The president can put you on the payroll to teach political science and still make a tidy profit.

Both these situations can arise at small colleges, but they are a bit chancy. It is far better to send out letters of inquiry to colleges, accompanied by glowing recommendations from colleagues and division chairmen.

In this connection, you will be helped immensely if you have done your undergraduate work at Harvard. Small, young liberal arts colleges simply do not get that many Harvard graduates on their faculties. Landing one is not only a social novelty but a prestige item for the catalogue. However, if you have attended a less important university, don't be discouraged. This fact may save you from a constant question which your new colleagues would ask: "If you graduated from Harvard, why in hell did you choose this dump?"

At any rate, the law of student supply and classroom space being what it is, you will soon get a job. Your Ph.D. will guarantee this. To most presidents, it shows that you are not only a scholar but a born teacher.

The Day You Report for Work

The day you report for work, you probably will be given a tour of the campus by the chairman of your division. Division is apt to be somewhat tweedy, preferring to think of himself as a transplanted Oxford don who is doing both you and the college a favor by being present. He is certain to ask you the title of your Ph.D. thesis. However, he is only doing this to be polite, so don't get excited and start filling him in with the details. More than likely, Division will be a kindly man, and you will be able to imagine him holding a class of undergraduates spellbound with his oratory, wit and wisdom.

"The trouble you'll find with this college," he may say, "is the bunch of morons we've got for a student body."

You should not be unduly alarmed, because division chairmen know it is expected of them to say this kind of thing. You will quickly discover that the only persons on campus who rave about the over-all quality of the student body are the president, the director of public relations, and the director of admissions. Because they must deal with the public, the president and the director of public relations have no choice. The director of admissions is trying to justify his decisions.

Division will not waste much of your time talking about students, whom he considers vaguely necessary but nevertheless an interfering nuisance. He will, however, discuss your departmental colleagues. If he tells you that one professor is a "good man in his field, so they say," you will know that Division thinks his scholarship is suspect. For the most part, you will meet only those professors whom Division wants you to encounter. They are the ones who side with him in the raging disputes that take place in faculty meetings. Division wants to make certain that you are properly aligned from the beginning.

At some point Division will discuss the college's administrative staff. You will discover that Division regards the administrators in an even worse light than he does the students. He can always flunk the students. He cannot fire the administrators. You will learn that the twin functions of the administration are to recruit stupid students and keep faculty members from spending needed money.

At the end of the tour, Division will take you to his office to discuss your teaching assignment for the coming year. Division teaches his specialty to seniors: "Cabinet Politics During the Lincoln Era." His associate lectures to juniors and bright sophomores on "Modern International Relations." This covers the period from the end of the Franco-Prussian War to the Treaty of Versailles.

"What about everything that has happened since then?" you might ask. The answer is, "We are too close to those events to get any true historical and political perspective on them. We would be doing students a disservice by confusing their minds."

You then find that you are permitted to discuss Modern Times in the course you will teach to three hundred freshmen: American Political History Since the Revolution.

More important than your teaching assignment is your salary. As a new instructor, it is in the neighborhood of $7,000 a year. This is certain to be insignificant compared to what you had planned to spend for the good things of life. No doubt you will consider augmenting your income by finding other work during the three months that you have off during the summer, the month off at Christmas, the two weeks during spring vacation, as well as two of the five weekdays on which you are not teaching.

But before you search the Help Wanted ads, you must go see the academic dean. He will suggest strongly that you spend all your spare time polishing your thesis so that it can be published in a scholarly journal. He will hint that he would be even more pleased if you would expand it into a book.

While vigorously denying that he is an advocate of the discredited philosophy of "publish or perish," he will declare that the course of action he is suggesting to you would be good for the college, good for your department, and good for you. He will indicate that the more books you write, the higher your salary will be.

Don't argue with the academic dean. He exercises as much power over professors as you, in turn, have over students. One of the academic dean's more awesome powers is that which permits him to assign a professor to a grubby classroom or to a private office near the cafeteria kitchen. To avoid this, simply tell the academic dean that several leading publishers have expressed interest in your thesis. Then leave his office and hope that he will be too busy with faculty meetings to remember what you told him. If this is successful, you will be able to take part-time jobs during the summer and at Christmas time until the academic dean catches up with you.

Bricks, Mortar and Bulldozers

The moment you are by yourself, you should wander around the campus to size up your new home. If it is typical of most colleges, it will be designed outwardly as a series of unfinished buildings connected by layers of bulldozers. Never has so much money, both government and private, been poured into bricks and mortar as in the days of the Affluent Society. The theory is that the way to Better Living lies in Better Education. In the minds of many presidents and boards of trustees, the way to Better Education lies through pretty buildings.

These gentlemen are not alone, as you will find out. One of your colleagues in humanities will agree with his class that scholarships are more important than buildings —but he will protest heatedly to the academic dean or the president if his office facilities do not equal those of the chemistry department.

A professor of science who laughs at the pretentious furnishings of the language amphitheater will be dismayed if his private research laboratory is not as attractive as a friend's lab at Dartmouth.

Students, for whom all this construction supposedly is intended, will spend their four years of undergraduate life picking their way between the bulldozers and the mud. They will be consoled by the president, who will tell them in senior convocation, "You will be proud and awed when you return to this school in five years and see it completed."

Parents, meanwhile, will be impressed with the newness.

Many of them shop for colleges in the same manner as that in which they purchase a new car. When you talk to them on Parents' Day, you will find that they discuss the latest physical improvement with the same enthusiasm as the president.

All this being the case, it is best for you to walk alone on the first day and form your own opinion of the architecture and the bulldozers. Otherwise you will have the thoughts of your colleagues thrust upon you. Almost to a man they will hate the design of the new buildings simply because they are so tired of hearing the president talk about it. Their capacity for rational thought on the subject has been filled. On the other hand, you might find that your uncluttered mind likes what you see. If you tell this to the president, he will consider you a man of promise and astute judgment.

At the end of your walk you must find your way to the administration building, since that is where your ambitions lie. Do not be disappointed if the building is somewhat run-down; money for new administration buildings is hard to come by. A donor would rather see his name on a new library, which is higher on the scale of status. But although the paint may be peeling on the outside, be assured that the president's personal office is the most luxurious one on campus. It goes with the job.

"Yes, Sir!" Is All You Say

The president himself may emerge from his office while you are in the building. If he does, go right up and introduce yourself even if you have met him before. He has hired so many new professors for the current term that he will not be able to see the difference between you and the basketball coach.

The conversation with him will be brief and one-sided:

"Do you like the campus? We're very proud of our fine building program. Have you met any students yet? They're a great bunch, as good as you will find at Princeton. And we're particularly proud of our excellent faculty. Incidentally, have you found a publisher for your thesis?"

It is only necessary to nod a few times and say an occasional and enthusiastic "Yes, Sir!" Any normal college president wants his faculty and staff and student body to agree with him, and if you go along with this you will start your career on the right note.

Off in a corner of the building, surrounded by mimeograph machines and newspapers, will be the office of the director of public relations. He will give you a warm handshake and present you with a scrapbook full of press clippings about the college.

"This is the one we put out about you," he will say, handing you a story taken from the local paper. It reads:

"Dr. R. H. Jones, whose brilliant doctoral thesis on political activity in the United States Post Office has received wide academic acclaim, is joining the college faculty as an instructor in political science, the President announced today.

"The President said the addition of Dr. Jones to the faculty will make the college's political science department one of the strongest in the country."

Whatever you might think of the story, you must thank

the director of public relations and ask for a copy to send home. If you do this, you will have an immediate friend. Directors of public relations live in perpetual fear that a news release will emphasize the wrong fact. They also are bored by professorial complaints, and have concluded that the easiest way to keep indignant faculty members out of their offices is to avoid controversial statements.

If you are friendly from the start, the director of public relations will think you are on his side and will write a great many news releases about your activities. This in turn will cause the president to think that you are important, and he will look with favor upon any plans you have to advance yourself within the college.

You will find it much harder to become friends with the director of development, otherwise known as the fund-raiser. The director of development will regard you as he does all professors: as a money-spender rather than a money-giver. This is so contrary to his way of thinking that he may, at first, be unapproachable. He will warm to you immediately if you can think of some friend or relative who would be willing to Identify with the college.

If you don't know anyone in this tax bracket, leave the director of development alone. His time, which is spent in raising money that helps pay your salary, is too precious to waste on idle chatter.

Before you leave the building, you will meet the director of admissions. Most likely he will be escorting a prospective student. "Dr. Jones," Admissions will say, "I would like you to meet this young man who is thinking of coming to our college next year."

Turning to the prospect, Admissions will explain, "Dr.

Jones is a new member of our political science staff. His doctoral thesis, I understand, is a brilliant one which is provoking enormous controversy within the Government. He is typical of the kind of faculty we have here."

This sort of conversation indicates that the prospect is a B-plus student at least. If he were a straight-A specimen, Admissions would have hinted to him that you were a former advisor to the Kennedy Administration.

With Admissions out of the way, you will have met the major administrative officers of the college, with one exception. The one person not in the building will be the dean of students. He will be out with his flock, wondering if it is going to riot.

2

STUDENTS:

How to Identify the Species

Although there will be hundreds of times when you will wish it were not so, a college cannot exist without students. This is sometimes unfortunate. Students get in the way of faculty research projects, and they sometimes interrupt the smooth functioning of the administration. As a result, proposals often are made to abolish students. One suggestion, which came from an administrator, was for students to mail in their four years of tuition in mid-September of their eighteenth year. They would receive, by return post, a degree of their choice. A fifteen per cent premium would be charged for *cum laude*.

Like all revolutionary plans, this one has met with stiff resistance. Yet, from the standpoint of the colleges, there would be many advantages. For one thing, there would be no riots. Also, professors would no longer have the irksome task of teaching, or the even more onerous chore of grading test papers and reading freshman themes. They could concentrate instead on sabbaticals and faculty meetings.

Under this proposal, a college president would not have to worry about raising money for dormitories or student unions. Instead he could turn all his efforts toward bigger and better field houses and athletic stadiums, which would favorably affect his college's earning power and prestige.

On a more personal level, there would be no use for deans of students. Freed of their awesome responsibilities, these men could return to the bosom of their families and no longer feel overwhelming urges to kick dogs when they get home from work.

Perhaps one day this Utopia will arrive, but until then colleges and universities will have to cope with students. This is a particularly grim prospect for young instructors such as yourself. It is one thing to have been a student; it is something else again to have to teach students. Students go to colleges and universities to learn, but they resent being taught. This is where the basic breakdown in faculty–student communication begins, and you will discover it in your first class.

Confronting you will be indistinguishable faces—eyes, noses, mouths and hair, often lots of hair. The emotions you will see are suspicion, hostility, fear and boredom. These faces belong to students. Your students. Your hope as a teacher is that, armed with the knowledge and wisdom that you are about to instill in their minds, they will rush out into the world and abolish ignorance and other bad things. Yet many of them look as though they merely want to rush out of the classroom, and others appear as though they want to abolish you.

Gradually, over the months, lines of character will form on the faces; you will be able to tell them apart. Finally you will know them as people, and even invite some to your house for coffee and conversation. (Don't serve them anything but coffee until they are seniors and you are certain they are legally old enough to drink; otherwise you might get in trouble with parents or the state police. When they are seniors, you may serve beer and sherry. Never give them whiskey; it is too expensive to waste on students.)

To be a successful teacher—and, later on, to be a successful administrator and college president—you must learn to like students. You do not necessarily have to reach the point where you insist that your daughter marry one, although you shouldn't object either, if she does, because the consequences are her problem, not yours. Your relationships with students should be such that you are not hesitant about inviting them to your house for dinner. Most of your neighbors will not object, particularly if you hold the dinner party at night, when you can draw the curtains. Even if the neighbors do object, the truly liberal professor —which, it is to be hoped, you are—will hold the dinner party anyway. Just bear in mind that segregation of students from the rest of academic society can only lead to deep and unjust divisions which will harm you and the college community.

The danger is that you will be so horrified by your initial encounter with students in the classroom that you will be prejudiced against them for the rest of your career. To help you avoid this, we have prepared brief summaries of various types of students that you will meet. To read about students is to understand them. The journey to the unknown is less fearful if the route is plainly marked.

The Student Revolutionaries

Everyone knows the characteristics of student revolutionaries. If perchance you don't, turn on the nearest television set and wait for the news broadcast. What you see may either frighten or anger you. This is because you haven't met any revolutionaries personally. Once you get to know them, you will discover they are just like other students except that ideas are more firmly fixed in their heads. It is to get these ideas out of their heads that many college presidents call in the police with night sticks. This is not the constructive approach you should take to student revolutionaries.

These young radicals are deeply concerned with the state of the world. Looking about them, they see nothing but violence and false ideals. They feel that the older generation has let them inherit a society that is polluted, crammed with social and racial injustices, and beset by totalitarianism and evil wars. They want to do something about it.

"Well," you tell the chief revolutionary on campus, "that's interesting. I feel exactly the same. You and I think alike."

"You do?" he asks suspiciously.

"Sure I do. That's why I've gone into education. It's where, I think, I can best make a contribution to the betterment of society."

"Yeah?" he pursues. "If that's so, why don't you join us in our demonstrations?"

"Because," you say, "I don't think violence is the answer to violence."

"See!" he reports triumphantly to his friends. "I knew he was against us and everything we stand for."

This will mark the end of the dialogue between you and the revolutionaries. You will have been dismissed by them as a knee-jerk liberal, and you never will be able to influence their thinking.

Take this approach instead:

In your conversations with the chief revolutionary, agree that society can be reconstructed only after it has been violently destroyed. Emphasize the need for widespread nuclear warfare. Call for the employment of bacteria and germs. Embrace the thought of a holocaust that will leave nothing but a few men and women living in caves. If you are going to reconstruct society to rid it of its injustices, you must start at the beginning rather than midway through.

The revolutionary will admire your grasp of the realities and consider that your dialectical thinking is surprisingly close to his.

Next, wait until he makes a speech to his followers. Then, as he starts to talk, scream "Fascist!" or "Pig!" Get it going in a good rhythm so that others in the crowd take it up. Combine the two words so that everyone is chanting, "Fascist pig, Fascist pig, Fascist pig!"

After a few minutes, pause and let him get a word in edgewise. This is important. You must let him provide you with an excuse for further interruption. He is certain to say, "So this is your idea of free speech, is it?" Start yelling, "Free speech, free speech, free speech!" so that he can no longer make himself heard. Do this for at least five minutes; then stop again. He will say, "Now, my friends, you know what democracy is really like!" Chant, "Democracy, democracy, democracy!" until he is forced to abandon his speech in disgust.

The revolutionary will be delighted that you believe, as he does, that the Right of Dissent should be both maintained and extended. Because of your actions, he will respect you both as a man and as a teacher. You will have won his confidence by using methods that are far less harmful than police night sticks.

The Intelligentsia

These students, according to most professors, bring joy to teaching. (A professor in likely to say this while enjoying a late-afternoon pipe somewhere on a beach with his family during the three-month-long summer vacation.) The intelligentsia are the ones who understand, who will absorb your wisdom with little effort and preferably with no back talk. This, however, is often the rub. The intelligentsia can rebel as surely as the revolutionaries, but they do it in the classroom, where it can damage your ego. As bright young men and women, they feel the need to assert themselves at the professor's expense.

With an uncanny sense of timing, they can tell when you either have a hangover or are just rereading a lecture—

for example, on the political justification of wars—which you had prepared years ago. Then they pounce.

"That's an interesting point, Doctor. But doesn't it conflict with what Hegel said about the American Civil War?"

"Hegel?" you ask. "Did Hegel say anything about the Civil War?"

"Sure he did. It was in the required reading that you gave us last week."

It soon will turn out that Gustavius Hegel was an obscure Union private whose letters to his mother appeared in "Some Personal Tales of the Civil War," a book which you had assigned the class to read if anyone had the inclination, confident that no one would. And Hegel thought the army food was awful, which, you are now told, proves that all wars are hell.

Your immediate temptation might be to ask on the final examination: "Define Hegel's theories of war." The question would be aimed at only one member of the class, and you would blister him for his lack of logic, his weak grasp of the facts, and his bad spelling.

On the other hand you would find it far more productive to take an opposite approach. Open a line of communication with the young man, which needs only consist of walking with him to the student union and offering to buy a cup of coffee. It is quite possible that he will accept the coffee, thank you politely, and disrupt the class even more when he returns to it the next day.

If he does, ignore it and try once more to win him to your side. Buy him a coke instead of coffee. The intelligentsia are vital to your happiness, and efforts spent on getting them to like you are worth while. Bright students can be turned into teaching assistants: they can read and grade freshman themes; freshman themes are the bubonic plague of academic life, and the quicker someone can be found to take them off your hands, the better you will enjoy your teaching career.

The Apathetic

Most of your colleagues will argue that these make up the majority of students at any college or university. Professors usually blame this state of affairs on the admissions office and the president, in that order. (The admissions department reverses this order; for further details, see chapter 6: Admissions.)

The apathetic are easy to spot. They affect a slouch in the chair so sharply angled that the student's rear end rests precariously on the very edge of the seat. His shoulders hang over the top. This is known as the bed position; it permits the student to sleep in relative comfort while at the same time occupying space in the classroom and not being marked absent.

Sometimes, on opening day of classes, you might mistake the apathetic for the intelligentsia. For instance, discussing philosophy, you ask a student in the rear of the room: "Name a philosopher."

"Can't."

"Kant? Excellent."

If you are alert, you will note the sudden suspicion, the attitude of "What's he trying to pull on me?" that flits through the student's eyes, and you will know that he is a lost cause.

The apathetic do have one virtue. Few students are more adept at thinking up excuses for (a) not being in class, (b) not doing the assignment, or (c) missing the final examination. Many a luncheon in the faculty dining room has been enlivened by a barter of the latest excuses, such as, "I heard a new one today: He was skiing, and had to rescue someone, and they were marooned by the blizzard in a cabin overnight."

"Yeah," will come a snarl from the next table. "He was with my daughter."

Undoubtedly your temptation will be to pretend that the apathetic do not exist as human beings in your classroom. You will be encouraged in this attitude by some of your colleagues, who will tell you; "I've got fifty students, and only five of them have any brains. I aim all my lectures at those five, and the rest can go to hell."

You will discover that the argument has merit. If you had to teach to the lowest level of the class, you would provide only a mediocre education to those who deserve better. Sometimes, however, you will find that the apathetic are only scared—of both education and you. If you give them a little extra attention outside of class, you may be rewarded by a glimmer of interest in your lectures. In any case, it will not hurt to get the apathetic to like you and to trust you; once you have them firmly in your control, you can tell them that, for their own good and because you are concerned for their happiness, they should transfer out of your course into something less complicated. This way you can both get rid of a hindrance to your teaching and do a disservice to another professor whom you don't like.

The Shaggies

A botanist was known recently to have staggered through the hall of a science building, eyes wide, exclaiming, "I saw a bush today."

"A bush? You always see bushes. Botanists are supposed to see bushes."

"This bush was in my class taking notes."

Beards, particularly those accompanied by pipes, always have been a mark of intellectual distinction. There is something about a neatly trimmed beard which implies that its owner has read a book. The hair and beard of a shaggy, however, implies only lack of a razor and a bath. It is unfortunate for those required to lecture in a small, stuffy classroom that cleanliness has become associated with the Establishment and the over-30s.

If you want to get a choral response from a roomful of shaggies, you can easily do so with certain phrases:

"Kennedy."

—"Beautiful."

"Pot is good for you."

—"Beautiful."

"Your thing."

—"Beautiful."

"Work is slavery."

—"Beautiful."

"Peanut butter is better than pot."
—"Ugly."

The shaggies are the great non-conformists of college and American society. You will discover that this is why they grow huge beards if they are men and long, straggly hair if they are women; dress in identical blue jeans and shawls; wear sandals; and talk alike. This not only sets apart their sharp identities but permits them to spot each other in a crowd.

Yet don't be alarmed by these creatures. Many shaggies are perceptive students and interesting conversationalists. They also flunk examinations and complain about grades as much as anyone. It is a cruel world, you will tell them. They will reply simply. "But it shouldn't be."

The Jocks

Jocks can be among the most interesting students in class, because athletes can be great moralizers. Possibly this is because games signify good fellowship and clean living. Jocks usually do not hesitate to make their views known on many of the great issues of the day. Suppose you are lecturing on the American Black Revolution, and you have emphasized, with feeling, that America has not done what it could for the Negro.

"I think you're wrong," says the jock up in back. "The Blacks get a lot of money."

"Oh?" you ask. "Like for example?"

The jock's face lights up in triumph. "Black basketball

players get higher pay than whites. You can look it up in Sports Illustrated."

Few students have more academic problems than the jocks, and it is a situation not entirely of their own making. There have been, and are, many academically brilliant athletes on college campuses. But some of them have trouble with their professors simply because they are athletes.

Consider athletes. They are functionaries, as important a part of your college's scene as student unions and fund-raising dinners. If they are good enough, they will provide your college with prestige, money and entertainment, for students and outsiders alike. No Phi Beta Kappa bookworm ever packed 50,000 persons into a football stadium. And if the stadium doesn't hold 50,000 persons, the All-American halfback and his playmates will be able to pay for a new one if they win the conference title enough years in a row.

Who would ever think of holding homecoming in a science laboratory, where straight-A chemistry majors performed on bunsen burners? Returning alumni would not be motivated to part with their annual giving checks. Any normal college, therefore, sets aside money for athletic scholarships knowing that its investment will be repaid in full.

Some of the money the jocks bring into the college may be used to pay for the printing of the academic catalogue. This will describe the virtues of a college education, such as having straight-A chemistry majors performing on bunsen burners. Some professors will believe so firmly in these ideals that they will be willing to flunk out the jock at the first chance they get, since the jock represents a prostituting of the Educational Ideal.

They will do this after spending the previous evening shouting with joy as the jock scores 44 points in a basketball game over the arch-rival. Therefore, take this advice: either don't attend basketball games, or else treat the jock like any other student.

3

THE DEAN OF STUDENTS:

Techniques of Participatory Democracy

To a professor, the students described in the previous chapter are academic problems. To the dean of students they are social menaces. Since the average student spends eighty-five per cent of his time being social, as against five per cent on academics, five per cent sleeping, and five per cent rioting, the dean has more troubles than the professors. Furthermore, these percentages mean that the dean plays a bigger role than the faculty in the operation of the college.

This is why you should abandon the lecture room and move on to the dean's office. Ignore for a moment the fact that you wish to be a college president. Granted, being dean of students is desirable background for that job, but it is an important post in itself. As dean, you will be the primary contact between students and the rest of the academic world. You will bridge the gap between the old and the young. A competent and understanding dean, who recognizes that young people do have a heart and a mind, can help make the difference between pacification and open revolt. This in turn will mean that your impact on education can be greater than if you merely remain in the classroom reading lecture notes and correcting final examinations.

The prerequisite for the job, of course, is that you like students and that they like you. Most young professors do like students, and this should be no trouble, providing you keep an open mind about them. If, however, you become a faculty veteran, securely anchored to your classroom with the seat belt of tenure, you may begin to dislike students. They will appear only as eyes, ears, mouths and too much hair, and you will be too bored and uninterested to invite them to your house for coffee. Therefore, hop off the faculty wagon while there is still time and ask the president to let you become dean of students.

How to Apply for the Job

If the president has heard that you are popular with the student body, he will look with favor upon your request. Nonetheless, in your conversations with him, be cautious when discussing the good points of students. If you are too pro-student, he will be wary. Therefore, be sure to point out that you believe in strict obedience to all rules and regulations of the college and the student handbook.

Emphasize that you intend to keep the troublemakers under control. Drop a few key phrases, such as, "I want to run a taut ship around here," or "I may be old-fashioned, but I believe in respect for authority."

The president in turn will tell you, "Don't be too rigid" or "Remember, students have rights, too." In dealing with the president it is best to overstate your case. This enables the president to bring you down a peg or so, a role he cherishes. The president likes to think of himself as a moderator. By letting him be one, you will get him to agree with your basic ideas.

When word gets around about your appointment, your colleagues will react instantly. The chairman of your old division, seeing you take on administrative responsibilities, will stop calling you "Doctor." He also will tell his friends, "I never did think that fellow had the brains to be a teacher."

Some of your colleagues will say, "I don't envy you." Others will tell you, "It's about time the students had a sympathetic person like yourself as dean." Still more will spread the word in the faculty dining room: "I think he's too soft to keep the bastards under control."

The students will simply wait to see what they can get away with.

To deal with them effectively, you must change the image that you had adopted in the classroom. As a professor, you were an authoritarian figure with power over their grades and therefore their lives. As dean, you must be more pliable. Basically, you must combine the confessional qualities of a priest with the pop enthusiasm of a disc jockey. You must be both dad and brother. This means that you are willing to play baseball with the kiddies

but can successfully order them to keep off the newly
seeded lawn.

Invoking Participatory Democracy

The task of enforcing the rules, whether they involve
lawns or marijuana, is never easy. You will find, however,
that you will have fewer problems during the school year if
you invoke participatory democracy. Students are demanding a voice in their own educational process. By letting
them use it, you will create such a Babel that in the end
they will give the responsibility back to you and your fellow
administrators.

An illustration of this will suffice, since the technique
can be used in countless situations.

One day a group of White students marches into your
office complaining that the college is practicing *de facto*
segregation.

Possibly your first reaction would be to chuckle mildly
and show them to the door. You must, however, hear
them out. The students are expecting you to deny that the
college practices any form of segregation. To them, a denial
only means that their charges are true. (This is an odd
phenomenon that you will encounter in other stages of
your career. Perhaps it is because professors have taught
students that life is far more complicated than it appears
on the surface; this in turn has led many students to refuse
to accept anything at face value.)

At any rate, the chief spokesman for the Whites tells
you that nineteen Black students live in dorm one, four-

teen are in dorm two, six in dorm three, and none in dorm four. This lack of racial balance, you are informed, proves that the college is the slave of the White Establishment. The spokesman hints that unless there is bussing between dormitories to equal things out, students will take matters into their own hands.

You could point out that dorm four is for women, and there are no Black girls in it because none applied to the college for admission. If this approach is taken, the Integrated Power Movement will demand the resignation of the director of admissions.

You could also tell the group that the racial breakdown in the dormitories came about because every student had freedom of choice when it came to choosing rooms and roommates. This, however, would be dismissed as Typical Middle Class White Protestant Thinking.

While you are mulling the problem over, a group of Black students enters the office. Their spokesman tells you that because Blacks are distributed throughout the dormitories, the college is trying to abolish Black Culture by practicing genocide. The group demands that all the Blacks be housed in one dormitory.

You now have a real problem: If you do what the Integrated Power Movement wants for the Blacks, the Black Power people will be furious. If you do what the Black Powerites want, the Federal Government will accuse the college of violating the Civil Rights Act and threaten to take away its federal grants and loans. This will make the president very angry.

Your predicament is universal—how to find a solution

that will either please or placate the opposing forces created by this complex world.

One answer is to leave things as they are. You could then use the threat of expulsion if someone disagrees. The ensuing student explosion would create national headlines. While this might please the director of public relations, it would arouse the ire of the board of trustees.

Another way out is to name a commission. By normal practice, this would consist of one Black student, one White student, six faculty members, three administrators, and one trustee. The very fact that faculty members, administrators and a trustee are on the commission would discredit its findings in the eyes of the students.

There is one other method, and this is the one you should adopt. Tell both groups that they should work out a solution among themselves, using student government as a mediator. Promise them that you will be bound in your actions by the student government's decision.

Student governments at colleges and universities are of the essence of participatory democracy. They help prepare the young man or woman interested in civic affairs for the world outside the campus. Presidents of student government are chosen, in the best political tradition, not for their platforms but for their personalities. Representatives to student government are nominated not for what they will do for their constituents, but because they are the only ones willing to run for office. Campaigns are won not on the principle of a free vote, but on how many votes one machine can turn out for its candidate. Decisions in student government are made not in the pit of public opinion, but behind closed dormitory doors or at private caucuses held in the nearest bar.

When student government takes responsibility for solving this particular crisis, it will name a committee. The committee will appoint at least two, and probably three, subcommittees. Football games, examinations and the winter prom will prevent the subcommittees from meeting regularly. When they finally do get together, their members will recommend to the parent committee that a student convocation be held to discuss the whole question of the college's racism.

The parent committee will mull this over for several weeks. Its deliberations will be delayed by the Easter recess and spring examinations. Finally, having been divided on possible courses of action, it will vote to turn the problem back to the entire student government. Student government will label the affair a priority item of business, to be put on the agenda as soon as drinking regulations are thrashed out.

Soon afterward the school term will end and everyone will go away for the summer. When the students return in the fall, they either will have forgotten what the argument was about, or they will have a new set of demands and petitions. You can then start the whole process over again.

Always bear in mind that, no matter how bleak the situation may look at any given time, the school term eventually will end. This will enable you to keep your perspective. It also will help to solve periodic crises such as this one.

You will not, however, be able to escape from the daily confrontations between students and administrative authority that involve sex, marijuana and beer.

Unfortunately you will not be able to apply participatory democracy to these three issues, despite the students' unceasing demands that they be permitted to write the rules. Sex, marijuana and beer come under the heading of moral issues. You cannot trust students with moral issues. This is due to the concern of parents, prospective donors, and the board of trustees. Trustees insist that their college be morally as well as financially sound. Parents don't want their children to get drunk or raped or both. Donors do not want their own names identified with an institution that has a reputation for sex scandals.

This is why you, as dean, must handle moral issues.

Pretend Sex Doesn't Exist

There is not much that you can do about sex. If you really are opposed to it, you could urge that the college be converted into a monastery. This would be as effective as trying to convince students that they should not indulge in sex because it is popular with the over-30s.

Modern college students, don't forget, did not invent premarital or campus sex. While it may be somewhat more widespread today than in colonial America, this is not the fault of current youth. It was adults, after all, who not only discovered the Pill but helped bring on the Sexual Revolution by finding it commercially profitable in books, magazines and the movies.

Therefore, sex should concern the dean of students only when it interferes with the smooth functioning of the academic world. Gang rape, if publicized, is bad for annual giving. It may also have an adverse effect on admissions if parents of prospective coeds hear about it.

Your objective should be to control excesses, not to prevent sex from taking place. The punishment must fit the crime. Gang rape should be met by expulsion or a severe reprimand, depending upon the character of the victim. If it is merely a case of a boy and girl living together off campus, you can make an example of them by withdrawing their cafeteria privileges. Unhappily this does involve the risk that the arrangement will spread, since students always are seeking excuses to get out of eating in the campus cafeteria.

To sum up: Pretend sex does not exist. Take action only if the abuse is so great that it may get into the newspapers.

What to Do About Pot

Unlike sex, marijuana is illegal. Marijuana, while more controversial, is to the current crop of college students what beer was to their fathers and goldfish-swallowing to their grandparents. Students find it a release from tensions, so obviously your best solution is to abolish all their tensions and frustrations. This will entail a reorganization of world society, including the abolition of television, politicians, the atom and urban sprawl. In some instances it will mean finding new parents for the students. In any case, it is beyond your scope.

The fact is that you will have to live with marijuana until students become bored with it and find a replacement.

Some already have. One dean was approached by a group of students who complained that several of their cohorts in the dormitory were burning incense to disguise the smell of pot. The dean immediately issued an order banning the burning of incense in the dormitories. To his astonishment, he discovered that the offenders were burning incense solely because they found the scent pleasing. They quickly formed an organization advocating Incense Power, and the Dean had to beat a hasty retreat. Therefore, be cautious before you clamp down on such student activities. Careful investigation can save later embarrassment.

Since smoking marijuana is against the law, you should try to stamp it out and punish the guilty. One method of doing this is to have sudden inspections of dormitory rooms in the hope that you will discover packets of the weed. You can also try to hire a group of informers who will snoop on their fellow students. The students soon will realize what you are doing. Their tensions will increase. To help control their tensions, they will smoke more marijuana.

It is quite possible, therefore, that you will conclude that marijuana should be legalized on the grounds that this may be the best way to stop students from smoking pot. No student wants to be caught sitting on the steps of the student union, puffing legalized marijuana, and have you appear, smiling broadly and saying, "I'm delighted to see you looking so happily turned-on." You would deprive the student of the youthful joy of being a rebel.

If Only Beer Didn't Come in Cans

While marijuana does pose many problems, they are minor compared to those involving beer. You will discover that you will have more trouble with the beer drinkers than with almost any other category of student. Many college presidents will permit the dean to have his own way when it comes to dealing with sex and pot. The president will be in a constant uproar over beer.

This is because of beer cans. Beer cans are unsightly. They offend parents and visitors. Sex can take place in a car or a motel away from the campus. Marijuana can be smoked to the end of the butt. Beer cans have to be tossed either into trash bins in the dormitory corridor or else out the window. This means that the maintenance department must spend hours of its valuable time keeping the campus cleared of beer cans. The business manager would rather have the janitors more profitably employed, such as in painting the president's house.

Beer drinking would be condoned both by college administrations and the National Park Service if only beer did not come in cans. One day a student may invent a paper carton which, when crumpled and put into a pipe, could be smoked and provide a thrill. This would solve the disposal problem. If you suggest that the student present his plan as a senior research project, he might be able to get a federal grant to finance it.

Until then, you will have to live with the knowledge that the president will telephone you several times a week.

He will ask, "How come there are so many beer cans by the library?" The implication will be that you, not the students, threw them there. You must assure the president that you will prevent the nuisance from reoccurring. It does no good to say, "Students drink, you know." Presidents want action, not excuses.

The most effective way to cope with this problem is to use the student handbook. Upon receiving the handbook, most students turn immediately to the section on drinking. The rule should be phrased as follows: "Drinking is permitted in dormitory rooms, providing there is no disturbance to other students. Disposal of bottles and beer cans must be in an orderly and neat fashion. Abuse of this privilege may result in its withdrawal." The last sentence should be in italics for emphasis.

When you next see a mountain of beer cans placed adjacent to the library or a dormitory, call in the head of the student government. Tell him that you consider this situation an abuse of drinking privileges. Inform him sternly that you may have to crack down on drinking. He will spread the word to the offenders. If you have been firm enough, he will say, "The dean really was angry this time. I think he means it. If you guys continue to be so sloppy, none of us will be able to drink."

This will solve the problem. There will be no more beer cans around the library until the next fraternity or dormitory party a few days later. Then you will have to start the process over again. Rest assured that it is a never-ending struggle.

The alternative is to banish drinking entirely from the campus. If you take this step, beer cans will appear everywhere, even at your office door. The students will have placed them there out of defiance.

How to Avoid Charges of Administration Brutality

Furthermore, abolition would run counter to the current theory of education, which is that deans of students must cope with the Permissive Society. If you don't think this is a Permissive Society, walk into a dormitory and find a student who is resting his muddy boots on a clean couch. Ask him, "Do your parents let you do that at home?" He will reply, "Yes." If you order him to take his feet off the couch, you will be in danger of stifling his creativity.

But don't despair. There are plenty of other students around who like clean couches. Find out who they are and ask them to be dormitory proctors. The student with the muddy boots will react quickly when one of his peers marches up and demands, "Get your Goddamn' feet off our clean couch." Once again, it is a matter of turning participatory democracy to your own purposes. By doing so, you will avoid charges of administration brutality.

The biggest advocate of campus permissiveness is likely to be the president. He prides himself on keeping up with the times. He also wants to keep the students happy so that they will not hang him in effigy and damage the college's image. He will tell you that there is no necessity of enforcing all the rules. This, he will declare, is a modern generation, opposed to regulations. If students are opposed to regulations, there should be a minimum of regulations.

Having said this, he will tell you that he has noticed a

disturbing trend in the dormitories: students, he has discovered, are moving lounge chairs out on the balcony in order to sun themselves.

"Those chairs cost us money," the president adds. "If it rains, they will be ruined. I want you to enforce a strict rule against taking lounge chairs out on the balcony."

You have to obey the president because he can fire you if you don't. This, of course, is one drawback to the job. Knowledge that this is so will not help when you confront the students and order them to remove lounge chairs from the balcony. They will be angry at you, not the president, which is an everyday hazard of the dean of students.

Deans can take this constant atmosphere of crisis only so long before they seek other employment. Some simply retire gracefully to their own lounge chairs. Others rejoin the faculty. You should, however, consider the experience invaluable. It is perfect training for the next logical step of your career, which is to become an academic dean. Once you have learned to put up with students, you will be equipped to handle professors.

4

THE ACADEMIC DEAN:

How to Survive Interdisciplinary Relationships

Next to the president, the academic dean is the most important man on campus. If God is the college president (most college presidents enjoy this comparison), then St. Peter is the academic dean. The dean is responsible for managing the curriculum, controlling the professors, and making certain the blackboards are well stocked with new sticks of chalk. He runs the place, but leaves policy to the man upstairs.

When you become academic dean, a curtain will slam down, separating you from your former colleagues, on one side, and from the president, on the other side. The dean of students and the director of admissions may still talk to you and have you over for bridge; they are usually kindred spirits. Otherwise, your existence will be lonely.

There are several reasons for this. The faculty will dislike you because:

—You have joined the administration. Instead of being

a colleague, you are now a troublemaker who may impose rules. A general philosophy of faculty members is that any rule imposed on them is a threat not only to their academic freedom but to their scholarship. It may also threaten the rules they would like to impose on others.

—You have given up teaching. Abandoning this noblest of professions raises questions about your morals.

—You work an eight-hour day as academic dean, five days a week, with a month's vacation. The fact that you have voluntarily abandoned a twelve-hour work week in the classroom and given up the three-month-long summer vacation shows that your mental stability is disputable.

—You don't keep the president in line.

—You make more money than most faculty members.

The president, on the other hand, will dislike you because:

—You have joined the administration, and you look like a troublemaker who might wish to impose rules of your own that would contravene those of the president.

—You have given up teaching, except that you want to "keep your hand in" with a summer-session course, and you are demanding extra pay for it.

—You are supposed to work an eight-hour day, five days a week, with a month's vacation. But sometimes you leave before quitting time, take extra days off during the week to play golf, and somehow manage to squeeze in an extra week's paid vacation over Christmas.

—You don't keep the faculty in line.

—You are overpaid.

Considering all this, you can see how easy it is to

become an academic dean—not very many professors want the job. Still, you must lobby for it. The students will be on your side if they'll have found you to be a sympathetic dean of students. The students do not count, however, and you should not waste your time getting them to campaign for you. Instead you must concentrate on the president and the division chairmen. They will decide whether you should be in charge of the college's academic program.

It is not necessary to disclose your views on education to either the president or the division chairmen. They are not interested in your views; they are interested only in whether you accept their opinions. Inform the chairman of the science division that you believe, as he does, that there should be more emphasis in the curriculum on chemistry and physics. Tell Humanities that you agree with him on the need to strengthen the English department at the expense of Science. Promise Social Studies that your first priority will be to hire new professors for the government department.

Finally, inform the president that your biggest concern is to avoid unnecessary academic expenses. Tell him that you believe the faculty is big enough and in fact could be cut down in size.

All will consider you both pliable and on their side. They will support your bid to become academic dean. Once you are in the job, you will have the opportunity to reform the college's academic program. You will, however, be able to do so only until the president and the division chairmen decide that you have gone too far in trying to change the status quo.

What Do You Mean by "Meaningful" Curriculum?

Until that point arrives, you will have a certain freedom
of action. Your first task must be to review the academic
program to see if it fits your definition of a "meaningful"
curriculum. Hundreds of other deans have written learned
papers describing a meaningful curriculum. It will only con-
fuse you to read these, since few are in agreement.

Some argue that a curriculum should be based on teaching the classics. Others point to science as the path to
educational salvation. According to many other theories,
the function of a college should be to prepare students for
graduate school and a possible Ph.D. From still another
standpoint, the objective should be to provide a general
education which would benefit an insurance salesman.

The result is that most curriculums are a compromise.
They are defined as such in the college catalogue. A liberal
arts college thus becomes one which educates a student as
"a whole person, equipped to meet the challenges which
lie beyond graduation, and who can make a meaningful
contribution to society and his fellow man."

The president is fond of this statement. He memorizes
it so that he can reel it off at fund-raising dinners and
Rotary Club luncheons. It commits him to nothing, espe-
cially the spending of money. The director of development
does not object to it, since it contains no dangerous phrases
such as "experimental," which might frighten a businessman. The director of admissions quotes it often, since
prospective students expect that kind of thing.

The faculty interprets the statement to mean that it can teach anything it wants, including remote specialties. Students either never read the statement, or try to get around it. Sometimes this depends on whether they want a degree or their version of an education. To sum up, we can take the example of a student who complained to a professor, "This English department has no courses that are of value to me to live in the modern world."

"That's not true," the professor said. "You could take my course in Henry James."

"Henry James!" sighed the student. "I want something that's going to relate. Henry James doesn't relate."

"Oh, my dear," said the professor, shocked, "you are just a child of your age."

Those in humanities would agree with the professor. Those in science would say the student was right.

To be successful and well liked as academic dean, you should try to keep both the student and the professor reasonably content. Here we get back to the search for a "meaningful" curriculum. You will quickly discover why the ideal meaningful curriculum is one that doesn't offend anyone. Largely this means leaving the professors alone to teach what they please. In most colleges and universities, the professors still have more power than the students, and consequently pose a threat to your career if you try to meddle with their educational philosophies.

Tell 'em You'll Mull It Over

Yet you must pay attention to the wishes of students. Students always make their views on the curriculum known, either through (a) private and enjoyable conferences in your office, (b) editorials in the student newspaper, or (c) violent and bloody upheavals. Their requests for changes usually involve total abolition of grades and examinations, coupled with requests that the practice of taking attendance in class be dropped, plus demands that the curriculum be made more meaningful.

Faculty members either (a) resist these demands with gusto if they concern their own courses, or (b) embrace them with affection if the changes involve someone else's classes.

How, then, can you tinker with the curriculum without getting some faction angry? It can be done, but the methods are complex.

To illustrate: One day a group of students approaches you with a request for a new political science course. They tell you that they all live in cities and would like to be taught about urban affairs. This appeals to you. An understanding of the crisis in the cities is crucial to anyone living in modern American society. It seems as educationally appropriate for political science students to learn about urban affairs as it does for scientists to study microbiology.

Despite your private enthusiasm for the project, you must be lukewarm while discussing it with the students. Tell them, "I don't think that course would be a good one. It's too specific. It doesn't lend itself to historical analysis. It would be difficult to approach it through the scientific method. Besides, I don't think we have any books on urban affairs in the library."

Then, acting reluctant, let them know that you will "mull it over."

A Course in Campus Warfare

If the students thought you were eager, they would try immediately to get you to adopt more courses of their choosing. Being cautious gives you a way out. Otherwise you might be asked to institute a course in "Techniques of Campus Warfare." Pretty soon students would get the impression that their views counted when it came to the college's curriculum. This would lead to many dangers and countless battles with the faculty, all of which would be disastrous for you, since the academic dean would be blamed for whatever ill befell the losing side.

However, in this age of participatory democracy, it is permissible for the academic dean to try to slip at least one student-suggested course into the curriculum.

Your first step is to take the idea to the faculty curriculum committee. Here it either will blossom forth into a catalogue item or be stillborn. The curriculum committee, the Rules Committee of coursedom, is licensed by the faculty to practice intellectual euthanasia on subjects which it considers academically unhealthful.

You can never be pushy when dealing with the curriculum committee, which considers itself more important than the academic dean. In this particular case, you must be extremely delicate with the chairman of the social studies division, since urban affairs would fall under his jurisdiction.

Take a copy of *The New York Times* to the meeting. Then draw everyone into a discussion of the news on the front pages. These stories are certain to involve either up-risings in the slums, air and water pollution, or a garbage strike.

In a conversational tone, point out, "It must be hell to live in the cities now." The chairman of social studies, who owns a large house in the country, agrees heartily.

Say offhandedly, "I understand a lot of colleges are teaching courses in urban affairs these days; I suppose that's all right in its way, but it seems a waste of time to me."

"Oh, I don't know," Social Studies demurs. "It's not too bad an idea considering the importance of the city structure in the socioeconomic framework of contemporary political society."

You can agree with Social Studies, but do it hesitantly. Then say, "I'm sure it is fine for those bigger colleges, but of course it would be beyond our resources here."

Social Studies is indignant. "The hell with that. We can get a staff here that could teach anything. As a matter of fact, I think we'll institute that course next fall." Thus, to show his disdain for the opinions of the academic dean, he sponsors the urban affairs course and argues its merits before the rest of the curriculum committee.

It is obvious, however, that the chairman of the science division is disturbed about the turn events have taken.

"It would be in your division, wouldn't it?" he asks Social Studies.

"Naturally. Why wouldn't it be?" Social Studies replies.

Science frowns. "The trouble," he says, "is that you social studies people are calling everything a 'science' nowdays, and I was a bit afraid you would try to palm it off on me. My budget is too tight already."

Social Studies flares, and for the next two hours there is a bitter argument throughout the room over the definition of "science." The chairman of the humanities division is in the middle of the fight, but for personal reasons having nothing to do with definitions. His hope is to prolong discussion so that everyone will forget about urban affairs. In the first place, he can find no relevance between urban affairs and the avowed purpose of a liberal arts college, which is to educate the Whole Man through intensive study of literature. More importantly, he fears that a new professor will have to be hired to handle the urban affairs course, and this, he knows, might doom his chances of getting another man in English for "Symbolism in Chaucer."

You will see that the tide is running against urban affairs, particularly since Social Studies is too preoccupied with defending his division to pay attention to academic matters. Now you must step into the fray. Point out that it is getting late. Mention the cocktail hour. This will bring everyone's attention back to matters at hand. Then suggest that the whole question of the new course be discussed by the entire faculty at its next meeting. This will free the curriculum committee from the heavy responsibility of making a quick decision. Furthermore, it will let everyone go home. Then you will have time to marshal the forces necessary to get urban affairs adopted.

The Faculty Meeting

Ordinary mortals, such as the President of the United States and housewives, do not attend faculty meetings. Be sure to remember this the next time someone expresses envy at the academic way of life. Point out that the President of the United States is free to conduct affairs of state, such as wars and political campaigns, and housewives have time to buy clothes and raise children, because they do not exhaust themselves physically and mentally at faculty meetings.

When you first attend a faculty meeting, you might be tempted to idealize it. It is, after all, a gathering of the most brilliant minds in the college. The professors are using the faculty meeting as a forum for the free exchange of ideas in the academic market place. They share the common purpose of achieving an educational goal that will be of vast benefit to the academic community.

Your first shock will come as you look about the room as the professors assemble. With the exception of one man, the first six rows are empty. The exception is a young instructor in English who feels shaky about his future in the college. He wants to sit close to the front in order to be seen laughing at the president's jokes.

The rest of the faculty are ranged disdainfully in the back of the room. There they have the freedom to exchange snide remarks about the president's jokes without being overheard.

In one section are all the science professors, grouped

by department. In another are the humanities, similarly seated. The coaches are teamed in an inconspicuous corner of the room where they can exchange snide remarks not only about the president but about the rest of the faculty as well. The reason for this grouping is protection, man's ancient herd instinct when in danger. Should either Humanities or Social Studies attack Science, then the scientists can call a quick huddle and come up with a spokesman and a vicious reply. And so on.

Students, with their inbred horror of being known by their peers as a "teacher's pet," also sit as far as possible from the front of the classroom. Professors consider this a personal insult to their dissemination of knowledge and demand that "everyone move up front."

Should the academic dean adopt a similar tactic and insist that his brethren vacate the back rows, there would be cries of alarm, mutters of "who in hell does he think he is?" and total refusal to do as asked. In fact, this would be considered an infringement upon academic freedom. Therefore, as academic dean, you must let the faculty sit where it pleases, even if it means shouting to make yourself heard in the rear.

The first order of business is to get the faculty members to stop talking, so the meeting can get underway. This task is accomplished in anything from five to thirty minutes, depending upon how much gossip is left over from lunch.

Only when the president begins to glance with annoyance around the room will you be able to call the meeting to order. Presidents normally look upon faculty meetings as a nuisance. They take up valuable time that could be spent elsewhere, either giving speeches or raising funds.

Furthermore, faculty meetings discuss academic matters, and some presidents have little interest in academics. Finally, the possibility always exists that someone might ask the president an embarrassing question. Presidents don't like questions of any sort, much less embarrassing ones.

The first item on the agenda is to dispense with the reading of the minutes of the last faculty meeting.

"Unless anyone objects, we won't read the minutes," you say. Expecting no objections, you start to move on to the next item of business. There is a disturbance in the rear of the room. You look up and see Political Theory on his feet shouting "Point of order! Point of order! You didn't use Robert's Rules of Parliamentary Procedure. You've got to make a formal motion to dispense with reading the minutes, have it seconded, and then voted on by those present."

Pleased that he has brought his training to bear on a live issue, Political Theory sits down.

The coaches groan. The scientists snicker. The humanists are disgusted, since the whole issue smacks of political arenas and the mob instinct. You are rescued by the professors in social studies, who must act since Political Theory is a member of their division. They take care of the parliamentary procedures, allowing you to proceed. You will now have learned never to take short cuts in faculty meetings.

Next you call on the president to give his report to the faculty. In most cases, this consists of two points: the marvelous amount of money that has come from annual giving, which will be used for the building program, and the exorbitant amount of money that the professors want to spend on academics.

"Take Care of This, Will You?"

The president finishes his report and sits down. In the back of the room, an English professor raises his hand. A murmur of expectation spreads through the faculty. The English professor is known as one of the most brilliant men on campus. He is a dedicated teacher. Publicly and privately, he has condemned the building program, arguing that the money should be spent instead to increase the library holdings and provide more scholarships for the poor. He has hinted to his colleagues that one day he may bring his feelings to the attention of the president at a faculty meeting.

"I would like to know," the professor says solemnly, "why students are parking their cars in the faculty parking lot. I couldn't get a place there either today or yesterday."

The president, genuinely concerned, rises to his feet. "You should have brought that to the attention of the dean of students or the academic dean before now," he replies. "I assure you, however, that I will take care of this immediately."

He leans over to you and whispers, "Take care of this, will you?"

You need only turn to your secretary and say, "Take care of that, will you?" She can then call the president of student government and order him to correct the situation. It is not necessary to get the dean of students involved. If you were to bother the dean of students at this point, he would only tell the faculty, "The reason students park in the faculty parking lot is because the professors are parking in the student parking lot."

This accusation would upset the faculty, and the professors would spend much of the afternoon arguing with the dean that they have a right to park where they please. You would not be able to conduct any further business at the meeting. Also, you would be late for dinner. Therefore, let your secretary handle the problem, and continue with academic matters.

How to Discuss Curriculum Offerings

With the preliminaries out of the way, it is time to take up the main business of this particular meeting, which is a discussion of proposed new curriculum offerings.

The first course to be submitted to the faculty for approval is "Plant Life in Hawaii." The description of the course that will be printed in the catalogue is: "A study of the varied plant life of Hawaii, with emphasis on its tropical nature. Lectures will be supplemented with field trips for an in-depth look at the relationship between plants and their environment."

You explain to the faculty that the course will be taught in Hawaii by the chairman of the botany department. Since he is personally popular with his colleagues, being one of the most experienced hands at giving cocktail parties, the course is quickly approved. No professor questions the academic and intellectual content of courses that are to be taught by a friend.

(The course, incidentally, was the idea of the president. Faced with a shortage of beds in the dormitories, he wished to send a group of students off the campus to make room for new freshmen. There is no better way of getting students off the campus than by arranging one or two "study abroad" courses.)

Now it is time for the faculty to consider the proposed course in urban affairs. Let us first review a bit of the background.

Two obstacles had been encountered in the days before the faculty meeting. The first concerned the question of who would teach the course. On the campus, there was only one logical candidate, a veteran professor of political science who had done social work in New York twenty years previously. This professor, however, is an overbearing snob who is heartily disliked by a majority of his colleagues, and a simple majority of the faculty is sufficient to get urban affairs rejected.

To overcome this crisis, you have decided to tell the faculty that you plan to hire a specialist on urban affairs from the outside world.

The second obstacle involved the chairman of the humanities division. As you will remember, he was opposed to hiring a new professor for urban affairs since this might doom his chances of getting another man for "Symbolism in Chaucer." In order to win his support, you have promised that next year you will let him hire two new English instructors, one for Chaucer and the other for "The Humor of Herman Melville." Satisfied at this arrangement, the humanities chairman has agreed to throw his weight behind the adoption of urban affairs.

All this groundwork has been done before the faculty meeting. Now the moment of truth has arrived. By prior arrangement, you call upon three Flaming Liberals, one each from science, social studies and humanities, to speak in favor of the course. They point out to their colleagues that an understanding of the problems of cities is necessary to the understanding of American democracy. Further, they argue that the course is "meaningful" to the students, since most of them live in cities. They declare that the course is in keeping with modern times.

The Flaming Liberal from humanities nearly blows the whole scheme by insisting that a black professor be hired to teach the course. This is too much for Ancient History. For ten minutes, he denounces what he calls the "suicidal academic impulse to knuckle under to popular pressures." Ancient History then makes a fatal mistake when he also insists that urban affairs are too current to be taught with any intellectual objectivity. This turns the science division against him.

When there is a significant drop in the noise level, you see that the time is favorable to call for a vote, but before you can do so the president stands up.

"I would like to point out to you people," he says, "that our budget for next year is extremely tight, and we are not capable at the moment of hiring a new professor. We can do so if you wish, but it will mean a cutback in academic expenses for the rest of you."

The urban affairs course is rejected, unanimously.

The Truly Diplomatic Dean

As you can see from this analysis, a primary function of the academic dean is to act as a diplomat who tries to achieve by peaceful means what various factions on the faculty and administration try to gain by open combat. The fact that many professional diplomats have served previously as college professors, or as academic deans, perhaps explains the prevalence of wars throughout the history of mankind.

You should not be discouraged when you encounter a setback such as the one described. The nice thing about the foreign service, as against the military, is that diplomats always live to practice their arts another day. In this case, you will have emerged from the faculty meeting in a good moral position to get an urban affairs course into the curriculum once the money is found to pay for it. The students, hopefully, will be content that you at least tried to do something for them. The professors will be happy that you provided an excuse for a good, rousing faculty meeting which will give them a topic of cocktail-party conversation for a week. The president, of course, will be slightly upset that you almost caused him to spend some money. Yet the outcome will have reinforced the president's opinion of his power over the faculty, so he will be satisfied.

Meanwhile you will have learned some lessons in the tactics of diplomacy. Nothing is more important for your survival as academic dean than this business of diplomacy.

The truly diplomatic dean, for example, always will keep

a spare typewriter table hidden in a closet. One day the head of the psychology department will come into your office to complain, "Economics has stolen my typewriter table." You then will go to see Economics, who will tell you, "I had it first. See, here are my initials scratched on the leg."

Now is the time to fetch the typewriter table you have had secreted in the closet. Show it to both Economics and Psychology. Tell them, "This new one has just arrived, but unfortunately I've lost the requisition slip and don't know which of you is supposed to get it. I'll let you decide between you."

This is invoking the same principle of participatory democracy that you previously applied to students. Economics and Psychology will have a furious battle over the rightful ownership of the new table, but it will be between them and you will be well free of the controversy.

The Teacher/Student Ratio

To illustrate further: One of your principal tasks will be to explain to students and their parents the true meaning of the teacher/student ratio.

To the president, the ratio, as the number of PH.D.s listed in the catalogue and the number of new buildings under construction, is one of the bench marks of Excellence. The ratio usually will be listed as 1:13, or 1:10. This is supposed to mean that one professor teaches 13, or 10, students, as the case may be.

The smaller the ratio, the more popular the college in

the minds of parents and their children. A ratio of 1:10 indicates all that is good in a small liberal arts college— intimate classes, highly individualized instruction, a chance to get to know the professor on a first-name basis. The hope is that this not only will insure better education but perhaps a higher grade.

Directors of admissions carry the ratio wherever they go, prepared to fling it in the face of a prospect whenever the conversation starts drifting to the University of Southern California.

Suppose your college has a 1:10 ratio, mathematically obtained by dividing the number of faculty members into the total number of students. The admissions department has used the ratio to win over a student from New York City who had attended a large high school with huge classes, and wanted a change.

On his first day at the college, the youth discovers that he is assigned to four lecture courses, each with an enrollment of 225, each with only one professor. He then writes a letter of complaint to his parents, who, in turn, ask the academic dean why the college is not living up to the catalogue.

The ratio is based on a false assumption. It implies that professors arbitrarily will be assigned a specific ratio of students—say ten or thirteen. Given the number of courses that all students are required to take, this is obviously impossible. In addition, the faculty figure is often incorrect. Some presidents obtain the ratio by filling the "faculty" side of the equation with college personnel other than teachers—such as librarians, half a dozen administrators who often are listed as faculty in the catalogue, and perhaps even the business manager. Since it would be unfair to the college's reputation to disclose all these facts, you must reply to the parents in this manner:

"Dear Sir and Madam:

"I have received your letter inquiring about the 1:10 faculty/student ratio. I can understand your concern, since some of the technicalities of higher education often are difficult to explain in the brief space allotted in the catalogue.

"Certain courses are required for all students. This being the case, it would not be economically feasible for the college to retain the professorial staff required to maintain a 1:10 ratio for these necessarily large classes.

"Please accept my assurances that your son will be attending smaller classes as he progresses through his education. Our course in 'basic microscope,' for example, has only two students to one professor."

Four years later, when this same young man complains that he has never attended a class with as few as ten students to one professor, you can rebut him with: "Did you ever take basic microscope?"

How to Dismiss the Academic Failures

It also will be your function to dismiss students from college as academic failures. This is one of the more agonizing aspects of the office, since there are certain borderline cases in which the process of making a fair decision is difficult.

There will be no problem if the student concerned is a shaggy who has compiled straight F's in his courses combined with a record of straight-A research into the uses of pot. No one will applaud the ousting more than the coaches, who do not associate beards with good sportsmanship and clean living.

Let it be a jock, however, particularly an all-conference jock, and you will be in trouble. The coaches will complain to you heatedly for up to a day. The length of time of the complaint will depend upon the particular athletic ability of the jock. You will argue that the jock's cumulative academic grade average was only 1.1, when it should have been 2.0. The coach will reply, with vehemence, that the only average which counted was the 22.9 achieved on the basketball floor.

If you wish to maintain friendly relations with the coach, who will give you extra basketball tickets for your friends, you will pass the ultimate responsibility for the decision up to the president. The president will insist that the jock be removed from the college forthwith. If he doesn't, the scholars on the faculty will condemn him for overemphasizing athletics.

"I'm sorry about this," the president tells you, "but we must maintain our academic standards."

As you are leaving, the president calls you back for one further conference. Naming a student, he asks hopefully: "Is there anything you can do for her?"

"No," you reply. "She made sixteen straight F's."

"Gee, that's too bad," the president says. "Her father gave us five thousand this year."

If you see an opportunity to improve the college, never waste it. Hint to the president that you will review the girl's grades. Tell him that some of her professors are sympathetic and may be willing to give her one more chance. When you have sufficiently aroused his interest, ask him, "What are you going to do with that five thousand dollars? It would go a long way toward hiring a new professor for that urban affairs course we discussed."

The prospect of keeping the girl in college, and possibly getting another donation from her father, will intrigue the president. He may accept your offer and let you hire the new professor.

If he doesn't, you can always flunk the girl for good.

You should not lose sleep over the scruples of this transaction. Colleges would be in serious trouble if they were administered on the basis of scruples. Leave scruples to politicians and student revolutionaries.

5

LOOKING UPWARD

When you reach this point in your career, it is time for a review. So far you have been concerned with students, faculty and academic affairs. These are the least important aspects of college administration, but an understanding of their functions is essential if you are to be a successful president.

Possibly you would quarrel with the phrase "least important." Students, professors and deans usually do. Their viewpoint is parochial. Students take it for granted that the college will furnish them with dormitories, student unions, classrooms and professors, as well as a degree. Professors assume that the college will give them students, library books and a faculty dining room as well as a salary.

What, then, is the "college," which does all this? It is the administration. The good administrator looks upon the college as a whole. From his vantage point, the campus includes buildings, cleaning women, press releases, alumni dinners, commencement speakers and the weekly payroll. His concern is management efficiency. That is why, to him, students, faculty and academic affairs are the least important concern.

Given this state of affairs, you can see why a good administrator is more important to a college than a good professor. The professor reaches only a small audience whereas the administrator touches everyone.

This is particularly true with the triumvirate of administrative power—the director of admissions, the director of public relations, and the director of development. The dean of students and the academic dean are, technically, administrators, but in a narrow sense, because they deal only with isolated constituencies. These other three officers concern themselves with the crucial aspects of collegiate life: fame and fortune. The man responsible for the most fortune is the director of admissions. Without him, colleges would lack tuition money, which is the one ingredient essential to their survival.

In admissions, it does help to have academic training so that you know what you are talking about when you tell prospects about the advantages of getting an education at your college. Anyone who has been both dean of students and academic dean will have little trouble convincing the president that he is a perfect candidate for the admissions office.

6

ADMISSIONS:

The Art of Filling the Barn

It must be emphasized first that no one on any college campus leads a more frustrating life than the director of admissions. Every spring, the president pounds on his desk and demands, "Get me students!" Every fall, professors pound on his desk and complain, "What kind of morons are you bringing in here for me to teach?" It is a wonder that directors of admissions don't wind up on skid row. Probably they would if it were not for the fear of encountering former students.

This introduction may alarm you. It is best, however, to be prepared. Far too many prospective directors of admissions approach their job with ideals waving like The Star-Spangled Banner. You will be saved many a nervous stomach if you go to the admissions office in a more rational frame of mind.

On the surface, admissions appears straightforward, a simple matter of supply and demand. The student market is

vast and ever-expanding, due both to the population explosion and the need for young people to have degrees.
Even if young men and women don't want to attend
college, their parents usually insist that they do. Many a
parent would be in social trouble if his child did not have a
diploma. Father's prestige would suffer among the crowd
on the 8:17 from Scarsdale. Mother would be so upset that
she would cancel bridge dates for a month until she found
a plausible excuse. ("No, she's such an independent soul,
you know, that, bless her, she's decided to work for a while
before going on to college.")

With so many people out there wanting a college education, you might think that your job would be easy. It
might appear that you need only leaf through the massive
pile of applications on your desk and select those young
men and women best qualified to attend your school.

When you do, however, you will find varieties of letters
from the prospects. Some will be mimeographed:

> Dear Sir:
> Thank you for your letter informing me about
> your college. I have received sixty such offers. When I
> decide, I will let you know.

> Perhaps another will say:

> Thank you for admitting me to your collidge but
> I'm not coming as I've been excepted at Yale.

Soon it will dawn on you that hard work is needed to
snare students. This is the first shock that many directors

of admissions suffer. You will find out quickly that you put in longer hours and do more physical and intellectual labor than many of the professors and deans. Don't be too envious. They need the short workdays and long vacations to recover from a year of handling the students that you give them.

What Does "Selective" Mean?

Most college catalogues have a line in them that says, "Admission to this institution is selective." As an admissions officer, you must interpret this to mean that the student should have a high school or a prep school diploma. On occasions you can overlook this requirement.

One thing that you must grasp firmly at the start is admissions policy. It has little to do with the written material in the catalogue. Only three factors are involved: (a) getting enough students to meet budgetary requirements; (b) getting students who will meet the academic standards of the college; (c) if getting students who will meet the academic standards of the college is not possible, getting enough students to meet budgetary requirements.

This, of course, does not always apply to the more prestigious colleges, the emphasis being on "not always." However, if you have accepted the advice in chapter 1 and found a job at a smaller, newer and less exalted college, the above policy almost certainly will apply to your school. As a critic said of one of these colleges, "Their admissions policy is getting more selective. Now they insist that the student have at least two lungs."

Your most immediate task upon becoming director of admissions will be to establish the number of students that will be needed to fill the barn for the next term. This involves administrative council conferences with the president, the business manager, the academic dean, and the dean of students.

The president and the business manager already have met privately to discuss the money they must have to pay for operating expenses. "I've promised I will keep the enrollment at 1,000," the president tells the business manager.

"I don't see how that's possible," the business manager replies, glancing at the sheets of paper in his hand. "We've promised to raise faculty salaries by ten per cent next year."

"Make it eight," the president says.

"Okay, eight; but how are we going to pay for that landscaping program on the south end of campus?"

The president nods. "I forgot about that. Fine, we'll set enrollment at 1,250."

Next, the president calls together his administrative council for a report. The dean of students is asked for an estimate of the number of students who either will be dismissed for social reasons or else simply vanish and not return. He guesses fifty.

The academic dean is then called upon to estimate the number who will be dismissed for academic reasons. His guess is one hundred and fifty.

"My God!" the president exclaims. "That's too many. It's not good public relations. It makes us sound like Dropout U."

The academic dean agrees. He turns a frosty stare on

you and suggests this would not have happened had a better quality of students been admitted.

You must now do your calculations. From previous experience, you had expected to have to bring in 300 new students for the next term. Now you discover that with an increase in enrollment of 250 because of the president's concern for landscaping, an expected social dropout of 50, an academic failure of 150, plus a graduating class of 100, that you will need at least 550 new freshmen to meet budgetary requirements.

Furthermore, you have just been told by the academic dean that the quality of these students must improve.

Will the Student Select You?

After you have digested this, take the rest of the day off. It may be your only vacation for the next year. However, if your mathematics is a bit rusty, you should spend the afternoon doing some brush-up work. This is because the admission of a student to any college is based primarily on an analysis of numbers: Scholastic Aptitude Test score plus IQ plus class standing equal prospective student.

Scholastic Aptitude Tests, or SATs, reflect the student's mathematical and verbal ability. The scores range from 200 to 800. A student can score 200 points merely by signing his name to the test sheet when it is given to him in high school. If his score is 198, it is best either to reject him outright or put him on a waiting list in case you run short later in the year. If his score is between 700 and 800, either it is a mistake or else you are working at Harvard, Amherst, Williams, Yale or someplace similar.

Class standing is an important factor in any admissions policy. A student who has a SAT score of 650 or more, with an IQ of 135, and who ranks 130th in a class of 142 is, in the terms of the trade, an underachiever who is not motivated. The professors at your college will dislike teaching him, and he probably will be a disciplinary problem for the dean of students. Deans of students dislike disciplinary problems, and, if you take in too many of them, you will discover that the dean will not only glare at you during administrative council meetings but most likely will serve you a weak drink should his wife insist that you come to dinner.

Letters of recommendation from friends of the prospect, teachers, and high school guidance counselors also count. It is important, however, to learn how to diagnose a letter of recommendation. A guidance counselor who writes, "Johnny is a personable, likable young man who is just now beginning to show his maturity" is trying to fob off an underachiever on your college.

Guidance counselors seldom write this kind of letter to the Ivy League colleges or to the other big ones around the country. They know it is a waste of time. The prestige institutions are inundated with quality applicants, and consequently live in what many other admissions officers consider to be a utopia of high SAT scores, outstanding IQs, and superb letters of recommendation. Yet the Ivy Leaguers have their own brand of problems. Yale, for example, must make certain that the students it wants wind up in New Haven rather than in Harvard Yard.

This, however, is a guidebook to success in a small college, and we must regretfully consign Harvard and Yale to the category of Disneyland.

As for your college, it is probable that you and your colleagues will decide that the prospects should have a minimum SAT score of 550 and rank in the upper half of their high school classes. This is a respectable goal. The president will be happy to accept this type of student, as will the academic dean, the dean of students, and most of the professors. Some of the faculty will fail to understand why all the prospects shouldn't have a SAT score of 800.

The operative question is whether these better-than-average students will accept you.

Many, of course, will apply to your college for admission either because its academic reputation is widespread or because their high school guidance counselor thought you had done a good job of educating his previous recommendations. Possibly word has passed through the student underground that sexual and marijuana activity on your campus are more interesting than the curriculum.

Occasionally a prospect will not only apply but actually enroll who will have a SAT score of 750 and rank in the upper one eighth of his class. He then becomes the "typical student" at your institution. When another prospect comes along for an interview, you can reach into your desk drawer and whip out the folder containing the details of the genius with the 750 boards. "See," you say, "this is the typical student we are getting this year."

You must be selective in your use of this technique, since it can be counterproductive. Looking at the record of the genius who may be his classmate, a marginal student may decide that he cannot compete and take his business to a college that is easier on the mind.

The Recruiting Safari

If your enrollment goal is 550 freshmen, you may be fairly confident that at least one third of this total will come in through the mail. You must go searching for the rest, which means haunting high schools throughout your region and perhaps throughout the country. The competent admissions officer prepares for one of these safaris as carefully as if he were hunting big game in Africa. The quarry may not be as dangerous, but it can be just as elusive.

You must arm yourself with Material before starting on the road. Material consists of the college catalogue, a brochure, and either a book of photographs of the campus or a movie. Admissions officers are finding films particularly useful as a recruiting tool. If they are arty, they not only impress prospects but hide the bulldozers. Furthermore, films can portray a distinguished professor with a beard and pipe delivering a lecture, with great animation. The use of a written commentary rather than actual sound can hide the truth that this professor, while the most intellectual-looking man on campus, is in reality the biggest bore.

Still photographs, while cheaper than films, have the disadvantage of holding up a mirror to reality. Many an admissions officer has stormed into the office of public relations holding a batch of photographs in his hands and complaining, "Can't you take a picture of this campus without showing construction?" The PR man's answer has been to politely hand the admissions officer a camera and say, "Goddamn it, you try!"

What the Catalogue Is for

If a film is good for the eye of a prospect, the catalogue and the brochure are good for his mind. The basic function of the catalogue is not to describe the college's educational program but to impress high school students and their parents. Make certain that your catalogue fulfills its role. It should have an attractive cover, easy-to-read type, beautiful photographs, a small section on tuition charges, a large section on scholarship money, and a Statement of Our Purpose, signed either by the president or the chairman of the board of trustees.

This statement should explain why your college's goal of educational excellence far exceeds that of any other institution. It should emphasize intimate classes and highly individualized instruction. The student/teacher ratio should be at least 1:10. At a maximum it should be 1:13. If it is higher, then be certain that the printer makes a typographical error so that the catalogue shows 1:10. Finally, the statement should say that graduates of your college hold leading positions in business and industry. There should be a strong hint that the United States occupies its pre-eminent place in the world today because your college helped get it there.

When you have edited the statement to your satisfaction, go and talk to the president. You must try to convince him that the catalogue's cover should be printed in psychedelic colors, possibly with subdued tones of coeds in bikinis. That is about the only thing that would distinguish it from the hundreds of other catalogues handed out by colleges to high school students and their parents.

The president, of course, will be aghast at such an unacademic suggestion. "What do you mean by telling me that our catalogue is just like everyone else's?" he'll demand. "It says right there in the Statement of Our Purpose that we're better than anyone except maybe Harvard. Just read that to them."

Why You Must Go to New Jersey

This will leave you no choice but to hit the road, where you can use your personal charm on prospects. The key to success on any road trip lies in the selection of the high schools that you will visit. Since you are a small, private liberal arts college rather than a state university, you obviously must charge substantial tuition in order to survive.

This means that you must go where the money is. Don't bother with rural schools. Money is in middle and upper-middle class suburbia. New Jersey is the happiest hunting ground of all. As a bedroom community of New York City, it is wealthy. More importantly, it has no colleges to speak of—at least not enough to handle the huge number of middle class children who live in the state. Therefore, go to New Jersey. You can tell you are in New Jersey when the prospects start to pant as you arrive at the schoolhouse door.

No doubt you also would like to recruit students in the ghettos. To do this, however, you will need adequate scholarship funds. The president will tell you that as much as he would like to establish such scholarships, he simply does not have that kind of money to spare.

This excuse will not concern faculty members. Finding the money is the president's problem. Faculty members think of ways to spend it. They will hold a meeting and pass a resolution demanding that the admissions office conduct a major recruiting drive in a slum area, emphasizing the need for equality and the necessity of helping oppressed minorities.

Your only reaction can be to tremble as you picture yourself walking into a slum school and telling the guidance counselor, "We'll be glad to take all your brilliant students whose parents can afford to pay $15,000 in tuition and room and board over the next four years."

How to Use Your Expense Account

When you finally do set out for New Jersey and similar points, you must be armed with an expense account as well as catalogues. The expense account is one of the most potent weapons in the arsenal that an admissions officer carries with him. It is not good business for the president of a college to closely scrutinize the expense account of an admissions officer when he goes out to hunt big game.

Unless you are a veteran in this business, you may hesitate at first to turn in an expense account with an item labeled, "Dinner for guidance counselor and wife and self—$50." But it is a legitimate expense, as we shall see.

A cursory glance at the situation would seem to indicate that guidance counselors and admissions officers have identical goals: the guidance counselor wishes to place his high school students in college, and the admissions officer wants to enroll them in college: yet, while the ends are similar, the means are in conflict.

It is fairly certain that most guidance counselors will have several students on their hands whose IQs range from 140 to 160, who are not only smart but brave, reverent, clean (an increasingly important qualification for admission to college), cheerful and trustworthy, and although All-Staters in football or cheerleading, have managed to be editors of the school newspaper, yearbook, and poetry magazine, while at the same time being president of student government and supporting their families by doing basic research on the common sneeze.

With this kind of student, all the guidance counselor need do is hand him the catalogue from Harvard, Stanford, the University of Chicago, and a few others, and send him on his way. The prestige schools want this kind of prospect. So do you. But the guidance counselor doesn't want to fork over.

What he does want you to take is another type of student: That is the nice young boy or girl who has compiled a straight-A record of blandness, coupled with academic grades of 20 per cent Ds, 75 per cent Cs, and 5 per cent Bs. Like his smarter counterparts, he also wants to have the benefits of higher education, which is to say a degree, but he cannot be accepted into any of the colleges that his parents want him to attend. The Ivies and the other prestige schools take this kind of student only as a one-shot experiment every few years to show how democratic they really are.

You don't want him either, so you ask the guidance counselor out to dinner.

"No, thanks, that will be too much of a bother for you," the guidance counselor replies.

"Oh, no," you plead. "I would love to have you."

"Well, if you insist," the guidance counselor says hurriedly before you change your mind.

He then telephones his wife.

"Honey, get a baby sitter. We're invited out to dinner again. No, it's not that same crummy college that insisted we had to go to Howard Johnson's. This guy says we can pick our own restaurant. Do you want to go to the Café de Very Expensive or the Chez Exorbitant?"

It is a pleasant social evening for you, breaking the monotony of the road trip, and the tab is $50. More importantly, over coffee and brandy you strike up an agreement with the counselor whereby he will make certain that a B-plus student applies to your college for admission. In return you agree to accept two Cs.

He has made three students and their parents happy, and you have taken a small stride toward filling the barn with acceptable enrollees.

(Don't inform the president of this agreement when you get back home. If you do, he will look sour and say, "Don't those guidance counselors realize just how good this college is? They should be sending us their As." Rather than be specific, you should tell the president only,

"I had a good trip this time. The guidance counselors really are impressed with what we are doing here. They're starting to give us some of their better students.")

The Dangers of Personal Interviews

If the guidance counselor is sufficiently impressed with your expense account as well as your college's catalogue, he will let you talk to the prospects themselves. You will do this either in private conferences or in large assemblies.

The private-conference route is the safest one to take. Here you will have an opportunity to show the student your catalogue and photographs, in the manner of a brush salesman displaying his wares. The secret of this kind of salesmanship is getting the product into the customer's hands. Once a prospect has a catalogue, he will open it and turn the pages, and he just might like what he sees. He then will ask questions, certainly including, "What are your strengths and weaknesses?"

The standard reply is: "We are strong in the social studies, sciences and humanities, particularly in modern languages, and our football team is always a winner. I do confess, however, that we need improvement in archaic languages, early Chinese history, and fencing."

It is in the assembly hall, where you can address the whole senior class and perhaps a group of juniors as well, that trouble can erupt.

Confident that you will win over a certain number of prospects by the quality of your talk, you run through what your college has to offer, point out the beauty of its architecture and the incredible proportion of Ph.D.s on the faculty. You also hit rather heavily on your Goal of Excellence and sum up with a ringing and rather nicely done peroration about the advantages of small, intimate liberal arts colleges, particularly yours.

You ask for questions.

A young man in the back row raises his hand, rises to his feet and says, "A buddy of mine went to your place last year and he says you've got an open sewer near the dormitories which smells and everyone always gets sick."

Naturally you point out that a new sewer system has been installed, which many experts have described as one of the outstanding sewer systems among the nation's liberal arts colleges. You emphasize that the problem not only is now non-existent but was greatly exaggerated in the first place. In the minds of the audience, however, the seed has been planted that your place stinks.

Despite this, one or two of the prospects may come to you afterwards and ask for further details about the college.

One of them might be the youth who inquired about the sewers. He may say, "I've been thinking seriously about your place. I hear they've got a real swinging student government there that is trying to get a lot of Student Power. Is that right?" Tell him, "No." Furthermore, inform him that you do not think your college has the right academic atmosphere for him.

This will be particularly true if he is wearing dirty blue jeans and sandals and is showing signs of growing a beard.

Whatever you do, take his name and memorize it. Then, if he should apply, you will recognize it and can reject him immediately. It is best to snuff out revolutionary fires before they ignite.

Meanwhile search around the room for a clean-cut, studious-appearing young man who could be a credit to your school. More importantly, he would be a credit to you. "See the kind of kid I'm getting to come to this place," you can tell the president.

Hopefully this will be a youngster whom you noticed in the front row of the assembly. He was taking notes while you spoke and seemed particularly interested when you mentioned poetry seminars and philosophy teas. He wore a tie, and was of gentle mien.

Get him aside, take his name, and follow up this initial contact with a phone call to his home and perhaps a chat in the evening with his parents.

Four years later, you will thoroughly understand the complexities of admissions recruiting:

The sewer-oriented beatnik interested in Student Power will have graduated as valedictorian of Harvard, will be a Rhodes scholar, and will be destined for a rich career of public service.

The gentle poet will have spent four years at your college organizing revolutionary cadres, storming the administration building, and defying the police until he finally was caught selling LSD and heroin and jailed for five years.

The Spring Deluge

Despite all your roadwork, admissions will only trickle along during the early part of the year. You will get perhaps a half or more of the 550 students you need for the September term. In spring will come the deluge. The prestige colleges and universities send out their letters of acceptance to prospects in April. The thousands of left-overs are then up for grabs.

At this time of year, many small colleges and students are in trouble—the colleges because they have not met their quotas, the students because they suddenly discover they have no place to go.

A valid reason for this exists. It is stubbornness. There is little wrong with it as a principle but it does have certain practical drawbacks.

Most colleges set high admissions standards at the start of the year and try to maintain them until the barn is filled with new students. For months, you will admit only those prospects with 550-or-higher SAT scores who rank in the upper half of their high school classes. You will be quite rigid. You will look at the application of a student who has a SAT score of 500 rather than 550 and who ranks in the upper two thirds of his class, rather than the upper half, and you will snarl, "Why does a jerk like this think he can get away with being admitted to OUR college?"

Then spring will arrive. All the good students will either have been admitted to your place or the one down the road. You still will need one hundred more students to meet the quota set for the year. Therefore you will have to start grabbing prospects who have SAT scores of 450, who had to repeat their sophomore year in high school, and who rank 120th out of a graduating class of 131. It also is quite possible that not even these lowly people have applied to you for admission, since they may have been scared off. Your stubbornness in being so selective at the beginning of the year has now put the college into potential financial trouble.

Students are equally guilty. They read the catalogues, listen to what their friends say, talk to their parents and guidance counselors, and then apply for admission to the prestige college of their choice. To be safe, they also apply to two more prestige colleges in case the first one turns them down. In the spring, all three turn them down.

Prestige colleges can do this because they have more applications than they can handle. It is a pity that everyone seeks to attend a prestige college—a pity, but not a tragedy. A prospect may not be able to enter Yale or Dartmouth, but he still can get a college education.

This is due, once more, to the principle that wherever a prospect exists, a director of admissions is ready to grab him to meet the budgetary quota for his own college. Therefore, do not be alarmed when spring comes and you still need one hundred students to fill the barn. American ingenuity has solved the problem of matching a prospect to a college vacancy.

In admissions parlance, this has been done through The List, otherwise known as a college placement service. For a fee, a prospect signs up with a placement service and provides it with his high school transcript. The placement service then compiles a list of its prospects; this is sent to colleges and universities throughout the country.

All the essential facts about a prospect are on the list. These include name, address, telephone number, name of high school, IQ, SAT score, class standing, and a category known as "course desired." This is to save liberal arts colleges the embarrassment of trying to recruit a prospect who wants to attend a vocational school.

In the late spring, the list is apt to be full of goodies— such as the brightish young man who confidently applied to Dartmouth, Cornell and Yale, and was rejected by all three. If you are personally persuasive, you will stand a good chance of landing this particular prospect.

The Personal Contact

Some admissions officers comb through The List, choose prospects such as this one who seem academically quali-fied, and send them a catalogue, a brochure, and a letter urging them to apply for enrollment. Don't use this method. Anywhere from sixty to eighty colleges will be doing the same thing. The youngster and his parents, not to mention the postman, will be staggered by the number of cata-logues that suddenly appear in the mailbox. The young man could select his future educational institution merely by posting the catalogue covers on the wall and throwing a dart at them.

Personal contact is the key. If you have an alum living in the prospect's neighborhood, send him around to sell the young man and his parents on the merits of your college. You must make certain, however, that the alum is a distinguished and successful gentleman who will make a good impression. You will be in trouble if the alum is either recovering from a hangover that day or else is a business rival of the prospect's father.

If you don't have any alumni living nearby, you will have to rely on the telephone. This means that you will have to move quickly. Otherwise the prospect will answer the telephone, listen to your opening remarks, and then tell his mother, "It's just another one of those colleges, mom."

If you are the first to call, you will be in a good position to close the deal. Talk fast, and don't allow the prospect too much time for questions. You should say: "Mr. Smith? This is the director of admissions at Mapletree College. We have received your name and your papers from the college placement service and are prepared to admit you for the fall term. I notice that you want to major in history. We have one of the finest history departments in New England. I'm having the chairman of the history department write you personally to outline your course of study. This is typical of the individual interest our professors take in students. I also will be sending you a catalogue and brochure. You will notice the photographs of our new dormitories. We're very proud of our new dormitories. I'm sure you will be happy here."

Before the prospect can catch his breath, tell him where to send his $100 deposit. Then congratulate him heartily on his choice of schools. He probably will run to his parents, shouting "Hey, I've been accepted at a college," and will urge them to send in the deposit before you change your mind.

Within two days he probably will receive telephone calls from ten other colleges offering him the same conditions. But if he has sent in his deposit, he's committed to you.

In this connection, it is extremely important that you

identify yourself clearly. One director of admissions successfully roped in a prospect during a telephone call and
then hung up. Remembering that he had omitted to tell
the prospect about the enrollment deposit, he called back.
"Thank God it's you!" said the prospect. "I forgot the
name of your college."

On other occasions, you may encounter this type of
situation:

"Mr. Smith? This is the director of admissions at Mapletree College. We have received your name and your papers
from the college placement service and are prepared to
admit you for the fall term. What's that? Mapletree.
MAPLETREE. That's M-A-P-L-E-T-R-E-E. You may not
have heard of us down there but we are quite well known
and respected in New England."

The only thing you can do about this situation is tell
the director of public relations that he obviously is not
doing his job. You will learn more about this in the
next chapter.

A Dead Cat in the Closet

The final stage in the admissions process is that of
showing the prospect and his parents around the campus
when they come for an interview. It is not one of the more
pleasant aspects of the job.

One of the first questions certain to be asked is: "How
come this place doesn't look as good as the pictures in the
catalogue?" The answer is: "We've had to do a lot of

bulldozing for new improvements since the catalogue was printed."

If you are taking a prospect and his parents through a dormitory, the father may sniff the air and ask, "What is that strange smell?"

"Pot," his son will reply without hesitation, and usually with a grin of anticipation.

Admissions officers claim it is a scientific fact that the time they choose to conduct a tour of the campus for a prospect coincides with a loud rampage by four of the dirtiest and most heavily bearded upperclassmen.

Another shaggy is certain to make his appearance carrying tools.

"Is that the maintenance man?" the mother asks with distaste.

"No," you're forced to reply, "that's the art department."

When she finally does see a neatly dressed, well-shaven adult, she cries out: "Well, at least part of your faculty looks decent."

"That," you explain, "is the maintenance man."

The prospect wishes to study history, so you hunt up the history department. As you walk into his office, prospect in tow, History is complaining loudly to Philosophy, "The students in this college are so dumb that I'm going to flunk them all out of principle."

As a final touch, you take the prospect and his parents to his future dormitory room. They had expected it to be in one of the magnificent new buildings shown in the catalogue, but you have to explain that those are reserved for upperclassmen. The dormitory you are about to show them may be old, you add, but it is quaint and intimate. As one admissions officer relates with a shudder, you then take them to the room, open the door to a closet, and find inside a dead cat.

7

PUBLIC RELATIONS:

How to Be an Image Merchant

A dead cat in a dormitory closet is bad public relations. Its presence will only confirm the fears of the prospect and his parents that your college is not as morally sound as the catalogue indicated. They would not expect Harvard to have dead cats in dormitory closets, and will tell you so as they are leaving to take their business elsewhere.

If bad public relations is dead cats, it also may be a marijuana raid by the state police, or a campus shaggy shuffling down Main Street.

Bad public relations are inevitable for any college. This is due to the presence of students. Colleges have had to overcome this handicap by establishing an office of public relations. Then they have gone to great lengths to disguise what they have done.

Almost nowhere will you find a "Director of Public Relations" at a college. He may be the Head of College Affairs in one place, or Director of Communications in another, or Assistant to the President in Charge of Outside Constituencies in a third.

Whatever the title, the occupant of the job is the college PR man, otherwise known as a "flack." His is a key office and one you must aspire to before you finally are trained to become a college president.

The reason for this is that the PR man's value to the educational system is greater than that of many professors. He must win friends and influence potential donors, inform the outside world of significant developments in his college that will have an impact on mankind, correct false impressions that may harm not only his college but the whole array of higher education, and maintain cordial relations with the various college "publics," whether they be townspeople, faculty, alumni, parents or the communications media.

This means that his responsibility is to get a story favorable to his college printed in the news columns of *Time* magazine.

It is unfortunate that the expression "public relations" has fallen into such disrepute, since this is an apt description of the functions of the office. An institution of higher learning cannot operate in a vacuum. It must have communication—i.e., "relations"—with its various publics, and the office of public relations performs this role.

Yet "public relations" does have an unseemly odor about it, due largely to the role of Madison Avenue in the Affluent Society. The term connotes the hard sell and the glossing over of truth for the sake of marketing an inferior product. Since these concepts are alien to colleges,

the office of public relations is called anything but what it
is.

In admissions, you will have discovered the importance
of publicity to recruiting. If you tell the president, "We're
not attracting good students because our reputation isn't
widespread," the president will declare that the fault lies in
the Public Communications Office.

"Obviously," the president adds, "someone is not getting
the message across to the people about our accomplishments."

Tell the president that you agree wholeheartedly and
that you would like to take on the job. He will be agreeable.
He is aware that the secret of quality education lies in how
it is described in news releases.

Don't be timid about your lack of experience for this
particular administrative position. Any good college or
university will have professional newsmen in its public-
relations office; often there will be more flacks in a college
than there will be professors in the chemistry department.
Your job as director is to give inspiration to the staff. This
means that you must constantly summon your helpers and
ask, "How many newspapers printed stories about us today?"

The Rise and Fall of the Eager Young Man

One of your assistants may be the Eager Young Man
who has just graduated from journalism school. He has
taken a position in the news bureau of the college at a
salary of $150 a week in order to gain experience so that
he can join a newspaper as an $85-a-week police reporter.

The Eager Young Man is to be seen everywhere on campus, pen and paper in hand, talking with students, professors and administrators. This he calls "cultivating my sources." Soon he is picking up confidences, tips, and legitimate news items which he can write and send out to the newspapers. It is good practice for the day when he will become a professional police reporter, where he must cultivate sources such as police desk sergeants, coroners and burglars.

Many of the more arduous news chores will be dumped on his desk by the city editor, otherwise known as the Director of Media Relations, otherwise you. One such chore will be to write "hometowners." These are news stories on the accomplishments of individual students which are sent, along with photographs, to the students' home-town newspapers.

The idea is to attract more students. If you flood a newspaper in Peoria with stories and pictures of young men and women from there who go to your college, you will impress prospects about the merits of your place for Peorians.

In some cases this technique can backfire. Suppose a story is sent to a home-town newspaper saying, "Joe Jones, a former student at Main High School, has made the Dean's Honors List at Mapletree College, it was announced today."

"My God!" will be the reaction of Joe's home-town friends. "Did you see where that dolt Joe Jones made the Dean's Honors List? That crummy college must be offering nothing but courses in sex education."

This will be an exception rather than the rule, and you

must ignore the danger. Therefore tell the young reporter to write home-town stories on beauty queens, star athletes, presidents of student government, and leading actors in campus plays. Whatever you do, make certain that you read what he has written before it is put in the mail.

Otherwise, you might come into the office one day and find him hard at work over a typewriter. "I've got a good story," he tells you. "The student newspaper has run a poll. It shows that while 60 per cent of our students have smoked marijuana at one time or another, only 10 per cent use LSD, and there are only two known heroin addicts. You don't get these statistics very often, and I'm sure newspapers would be interested."

Point out to the young man that your action in tearing up his story is not a matter of suppression of news or censorship. Tell him that it merely conflicts with the administration's findings, which are that not one single student on campus uses drugs. If he objects, send him out immediately to do a story on the accomplishments of a faculty member.

He will do this, since young reporters learn early that the secret of journalistic success is taking orders from the city editor. He will get in touch with the faculty member, interview the man, read the pertinent documents, and then return to the office. He will write a story in the manner prescribed by journalism school:

"Abe Lincoln had a false beard!

"This is the tentative conclusion of Dr. R. E. Search, professor of history at the college. He says the discovery may have a profound effect on current opinion concerning Lincoln's credibility.

"Dr. Search bases his conclusion on exhaustive study of contemporary accounts of Lincoln's appearance, including photographs, diaries and newspapers.

"Dr. Search is chairman of the college's distinguished history department and three years ago attended a history workshop at Harvard University. He also was a guest at a Yale summer seminar five years ago. Dr. Search received his bachelor's degree from Unknown College in California, and his master's degree and Ph.D. from Whose-heardofit University in Florida."

The story is then submitted to Dr. Search for approval. The Doctor is appalled. "Young man," he says, "you are treating this discovery too lightly. These things cannot be popularized in such a manner." He admits that one must "write down" to the public in newspapers, but says that he will take care of the news release himself. In a few days, he returns with his version:

"Dr. R. E. Search, Chairman of the History Department, professor of history, whose specialty is the study of the American Civil War, 1860–1864, with particular emphasis on what in the current idiom is called "The Credibility Gap," that is to say perhaps a disbelief in the spoken word of government, has recently published a paper in which he reached certain[1] tentative conclusions about the beard of President A. Lincoln.

"Dr. Search permits himself to assert that these conclusions cannot be based on scientific analysis of the beard

---

[1] " 'Certain' may be confusing to the popular mind. In this case, it does not constitute an overwhelming statement of belief, but is used in the writer's definition as meaning 'vaguely possible.'— R.E.S."

itself, which, unfortunately, is no longer available for academic study. In this connection, Dr. Search wishes to stress his contention that the National Archives does not, at times, pay sufficient heed to the future needs of historians.

"In his study of Mr. Lincoln's credibility as a public servant, Dr. Search came across a letter written by one Gustavius Hegel to his mother, which contained the phrase 'By Lincoln's false beard, we are hungry.'

"This, and the assertion of a Cabinet colleague of Mr. Lincoln's that the President kept himself 'razor sharp,' has led Dr. Search to a tentative conclusion that the beard was false."

As office director, you have the responsibility of deciding which version to send to the press. The young journalist argues that only his story will get printed. Yet you both know that the professor will be furious if his account is not used. He will complain to the president that you are infringing upon academic freedom and trespassing upon scholarship.

Your over-all obligation, however, is to the greater good of the college. This means getting its name in newsprint. In turn, this means that you must give the press a journalistic-style story that can be published. You can always shove the professor's version onto the back page of the Alumni News.

The next day, the local newspaper appears with the young journalist's story headlined on the front page ("Honest Abe a Fake, Prof Says"). While you are reading it, the professor enters the room, the offending front page clutched in his hand.

"What kind of dishonest journalism is this?" he says angrily.

Before you can answer, the president appears.

"Congratulations," he says to the professor. "Marvelous story about you on the front page today. That's the kind of publicity I like to see. I'll mention you at the next meeting of the board of trustees."

At this point, you must step into the discussion. "Professor," you say, "the paper now wants to run a picture of you. And I'm having them give us fifty extra copies to send out to influential editors. Maybe *Time* will pick it up."

The professor will be so pleased with the publicity that he will tell his colleagues what a fine fellow you are. For weeks afterwards, other professors will hand you obscure research papers on even more obscure topics and tell you, "I think this would make a good front-page article."

Meanwhile the young reporter will be turning out a press release a day. To the delight of Geology, he writes a lengthy dispatch on the nature of rocks that will be seen when the geology department takes its students on a field trip to the nearby sewage-disposal area. But the local newspaper will not consider this piece newsworthy and will fail to print it, running in its place a dispatch on the latest Presidential election.

The Rise and Fall of the Old, Experienced Newspaperman

The geology department will consider this the reporter's fault and will complain to the president that it is not being treated fairly by the public relations office. The president will call you in for a conference and ask what should be done to rectify the situation. You should point out that the young reporter is inexperienced. Tell the president that you have tried to correct his faults, but have concluded that they are uncorrectible. Then suggest to the president that the young reporter be replaced by a veteran newspaperman who really knows his way around the city rooms.

The president will be delighted with this idea—again on the theory that if the college is not getting national publicity, it must be someone's fault.

The Old Newspaperman will then be hired. He has served twenty-five years on the city desk of a New York newspaper, and has decided to leave the big time for the leisurely, intellectual pace of the academic world. Fortunately for the catalogue, he did attend college, where he had obtained a bachelor's degree, which appears in print as a master's due to a typographical error by the printer.

You can leave the Old Newspaperman alone. He knows his job better than you do. Besides, the president will have certain ideas on publicity which he will convey directly to the Old Newspaperman. The president, in fact, will consider the function of the Old Newspaperman to be a complete remapping of the direction that has been taken by your public relations department.

This means that he is to place news of the college in *The New York Times* for a starter, and then *Time* and *Life* magazines, rather than in the local newspaper, as you have been doing.

After the Old Newspaperman's first week on the job, the president strolls into his office, a copy of *Time* in hand.

"Did you see the story on Columbia University in the education section of *Time* this week?" the president inquires.

The Old Newspaperman admits that he did.

"I think we have a story to tell that is just as good as Columbia's which should be in the education section," the president adds.

"But," the Old Newspaperman protests, "that story on Columbia was about a riot!"

"I'm not suggesting that our story be about a riot," the president adds testily. "What I had in mind was something favorable to us."

The president then points out that the geology department has been taking its students on field trips to the local sewage-disposal area. He emphasizes how this demonstrates the college's concern for anti-pollution measures. He declares that pollution is newsworthy these days, and suggests that the education editor of *Time* undoubtedly would be interested.

When the Old Newspaperman expresses skepticism, the president says, "You were in that business for twenty-five years. You know all those people. All you have to do is call up your friends and tell them to print a story about us. Why do you think you were hired?"

The Old Newspaperman reluctantly telephones a friend on *Time*.

"John? This is Henry."

"Henry! Hey, I've heard you've got out of the rat race and gone to the ivory tower. Gee, I sure do envy you. I wish I had the guts to make a break like that. What's it like?"

"Fascinating, a real change. We're doing all sorts of things up here at the college. We've even got an anti-pollution program going."

"Anti-pollution on a college campus? That's crazy. I thought only New York was polluted. You better watch out or some clown at your place will think it's important and will want you to write a story about it. I've got to go now—I'm doing the cover story on the war. Do you miss the news that really counts? Come and see me when you get to New York. Bye, now."

Although *Time* is not interested in the story, the local television station is. It sends out a film crew to do a one-minute clip on the geology students searching through rubbish for schist. The day after it appears, the Old Newspaperman gets a call from the director of media at a nearby college.

"My president saw that film on your college on the 11 p.m. news last night," the colleague explains. "Now he is demanding equal time. Can you give me the name of the contact that you have at the station?"

Tell the Old Newspaperman that he must not do so. If he does, your president will see whatever film is produced about the rival college, and the cycle will start anew.

The downfall of the Old Newspaperman comes when he is asked to do a news release on a forthcoming evening of culture at the college. He writes, "An evening of musical entertainment will be combined with a showing of student art at the college this Thursday. The public is invited."

The director of music comes by, reads the news release, and offers one small suggestion: The first paragraph should say, "An outstanding evening of musical entertainment will be held at the college this Thursday." The art show, he adds, can be mentioned in the last paragraph, if at all.

A short time later the chairman of the art department drops into the office. His suggestion is that the story say, "An outstanding show of paintings by the college's talented artists will be held this Thursday." The musical entertainment, he adds, can be mentioned in the last paragraph, if at all.

When the Old Newspaperman refuses to change his original story, both Art and Music complain to the president. The president, who must try to keep faculty members happy, insists that separate news releases be written about the two events. His opinion is that this would be a better procedure because two stories, instead of one, would appear in the local paper, giving twice as much publicity to the college.

The local newspaper gets both accounts. It does not have room to print them, so writes one story about the two events and says, "An evening of musical entertainment will be combined with a showing of student art at the college this Thursday. The public is invited." In the rewriting, the names of both the director of music and the chairman of art are misspelled, and the wrong location is given. The Old Newspaperman is blamed by the president. He returns to journalism, vowing never to read or write another story about colleges.

The Rise and Fall of the Professional PR Man

You and the president, meanwhile, will search for someone else to produce the fame which the president knows the college deserves. For the new approach, he will want to turn to the Professional Public Relations Man.

The Professional comes to the campus from his New York office for three days on an expense account, permits the president to put him up free at a motel and provide all meals, and searches for something to sell. He does not bother with the academic program, since that is dull and has a low promotion content, nor does he pause long to consider the students, who are not merchandisable values. He does pay attention to the architecture, which can be photographed, and to the president, who is paying his bills.

The idea he conceives involves staging a circus on the mall between the library and the engineering building, with baboons and giraffes sporting college beanies, a monkey painting an abstract portrait, elephants playing football, and the president performing as a clown.

"This way we can put across the idea that education at your place is a fun process," he explains eagerly. "I'm sure *Life* will take pictures."

The president is dubious, but is sufficiently intrigued about having *Life* photographers on campus to take the idea to the board of trustees. The trustees mull it over and produce a compromise: there should be no circus, but *Life* should come anyway.

The Professional shrugs his shoulders and goes out to get *Life*. He spends two thousand dollars of the college's money on the entertainment of the magazine's editors, who, to get rid of him, agree to send a reporter and photographer to the campus to see if there really is a story.

What they find so astounds them that the resulting exposé of the college's permissive attitude toward students and its shoddy academic program is the talk of the nation for a week. It also boosts admissions applications by fifty per cent.

How to Do It Yourself

The techniques of publicity we have discussed so far have involved the use of professionals outside the academic field. There is no specific course in most college catalogues, with the exception of those a few schools of communications, to show you how the game is played. But don't be alarmed if the president suddenly calls you into his office and dumps all the chores of public relations, including the trivia, onto you. He is likely to do this after the failure of various attempts to achieve favorable national publicity. "I don't see why we are wasting money on experts when you could do the job yourself," he will tell you.

The public-relations methods you should now adopt are simple, and have been perfected by the White House. They center on the theory that all good news originates with the president. All bad news does not happen, or else is the fault of the other party. Favorable events are publicized endlessly. Awkward news is a distortion of the truth.

Thus, you could use the following outline for news releases of almost any occasion:

JUNE

President Goodnoose announced today that a $6.7 million arts and crafts building, certain to be the most beautiful in the state, will be built at the college starting next month.

Dr. Goodnoose, one of the country's leading educators, said, "This magnificent building will be an architectural masterpiece which will be the pride of all. It also will make our arts and crafts program equal to that of any college in the country."

JULY

President Goodnoose announced today that construction of a $6.7 million arts and crafts building, certain to be the most beautiful in the state, will start at the college in a few days.

AUGUST

President Goodnoose announced that construction started at the college today on a spectacular $6.7 million arts and crafts building.

DECEMBER

President Goodnoose announced today that construction is proceeding according to plan on a $6.7 million arts and crafts building at the college.

"I say in all honesty that it will be as good as Lincoln Center," the president declared.

NEXT JULY

President Goodnoose announced today that a $6.7 million arts and crafts building, hailed as one of the finest of its kind in the world, will be formally opened at the college next week.

By now you have made the most out of blueprints and bulldozers. If the governor won't come to dedicate the building, he is not up for re-election.

In addition, you must have the president announce every donation to the college, whether it be a National Science Foundation grant of $500 to a professor (in this case, it is best to omit the figure) or a $1 million gift by an alumnus who is going to have a building named in his honor. The hope here is that "contagion psychology" will seize the populace, making everyone want to contribute to annual giving. People prefer to give to the winning side, which is why Harvard gets more money than you do.

What the president does not announce is bad news. If two students are arrested for holding up the local bank, it is the dean of students who tells newspapermen that the college's reaction is one of shock, and that both students were about to be dismissed anyway because they did not measure up to the institution's ideals.

When the football team loses for two straight years, it is the coach, and not the president, who must make the alibis to newspapermen. The president's role is reserved for congratulating the coach when the team wins the championship, and for announcing the hiring of a new coach after he has fired the old one.

How to Befog Bad News and Neutralize Enemies

To illustrate the technique of befogging bad news, let us suppose that the state police have uncovered a sex ring operated out of the dormitories by a group of students.

The president's first reaction will be that you should deny everything when the reporters telephone for an official statement from the college. This is true of presidents whether they are heads of colleges, of corporations, or of the United States. In this case, the denial will not work since the record of the raid will have been written in the police blotter for the eyes of prying newsmen to see.

What you can do is insist that whatever appears in the newspaper is a "complete distortion of the facts." This makes it sound as though the press were at fault.

Next, you should send the newspapers a list of new faculty members. Hopefully most of these will be Phi Beta Kappas or Rhodes scholars. The idea is to nullify sex by emphasizing academics. A good public-relations man will save a Phi Beta Kappa announcement for just such emergencies.

The next step is to consult with student government and have it organize a quick blood-donor drive. This will show everyone that your students are responsible citizens who love the townspeople better than themselves.

Finally, you should make a speech to the Rotary Club pointing out that the sex raid simply reflected a breakdown of morality in Our Society, and that it is up to parents to steer their children along the path of goodness and clean living. This shifts the blame away from the college and onto the Rotary Club.

These measures will help the college maintain good relations with its town. One of your most important functions as public-relations officer is to keep town and gown on as placid a footing as possible. In reality, the job here is not to win friends so much as it is to neutralize enemies.

It does no lasting good for colleges to dismiss the locals as dumb clods who simply cannot appreciate all the cultural advantages of an institution of higher learning. The possibility is always present that these same clods will rise up in revolution, and, while Mme. Defarge sits in the town square knitting, decide to erect a guillotine and slice off the college's tax-exempt status.

The tax-exempt status of college land is a sore point with all towns. However, the revenues that are lost are more than offset by the amount of business that comes to the storekeepers of any college town. Chambers of commerce are inordinately fond of a college in their midst, since they can write brochures which say they are a college town. "Isn't this a pretty little college town?" says the visitor, and the manager of the local chamber beams every time he hears it. Each such expression is likely to mean a clink in someone's cash register.

Town/Gown relationships in any community in the nation would be harmonious if it were not for students. Townspeople who take great pride in having a prestige college in their midst always temper their feelings on the day school opens and the Shaggies make their reappearance.

The shopkeeper who has just sold a student a $60 suit is perfectly happy until he finds the check has bounced.

Townspeople are flattered by the interest shown by the student body when it presents itself for the local blood-donor drive, and then they read in the paper the next day that one of the students stole the jacket of a state policeman who also was donating blood.

One way to counteract these bad impressions is to emphasize your college's cultural advantages to the community. This is done through the mailing list. To those on this list, you should send notices of all cultural events at the college, such as An Evening of Baroque and Atonal Music, A Show of Experimental Abstractions, and so on.

Anyone with the remotest connection with or interest in the college should be on the mailing list. Naturally, this includes the richest people in town. It also includes the manager of the local gas station. The theory is that any ill will he may feel as a result of a bouncing check will be overcome by an invitation to spend an evening of enlightenment at a lecture on "Geology of the Pre-Cambrian Period."

These measures in themselves will not be enough to overcome the weekly storms caused by students. In addition, you should mix as much as possible with townspeople who count. It is a good idea to pay frequent social visits to such dignitaries as the newspaper editor, the chief of police, and the mayor. If you are walking down the street with the mayor and you see a group of barefoot Shaggies, you can comment quickly on the poor admissions standards of a nearby college.

The mayor, a town booster, will be quick to pick this up, and will tell his friends, "A lot of those dirty bums you see on the streets don't come from *our* college, you know."

Most townspeople never visit the campus of their local college. You should arrange such a visit for people who count. Then, have the president and the academic dean deliver speeches on the services offered by the college to society in general and the town in particular, such as lectures. The best time to arrange such an outing is summer, when the students have gone and the maintenance department has been able to clear away the beer cans.

The Art of Snaring Big-Name Speakers

It also is extremely important for you to get speakers of national prominence on the campus. This will provide the community with civic pride, give townspeople an excuse for an evening out to hear someone famous, and create a cushion of good feeling for the next day that the students act like students.

The administration of many a college will spend more time during the year trying to snare a major speaker than it will on revising the curriculum to make it more meaningful. A major speaker means prestige. Should he be important enough, he will attract not only the local press but perhaps reporters from national publications as well.

It is not necessary that the speaker say anything relevant to the education of the college's students. No one consciously sits down in college administrative offices and says, "Let's have a speaker this year who will provide an intellectual contribution to the minds of our student body." The unspoken wish in the administration's mind is to provide Identity, i.e., Westminster College in Fulton, Missouri equals Sir Winston Churchill and the Iron Curtain. Glassboro State College in Glassboro, New Jersey equals Lyndon Johnson and Alexei Kosygin.

Not for years will colleges and universities throughout

the country get over the shock of having the President of the United States and the Premier of the Soviet Union choose Glassboro as the site for their 1967 Summit. "Glassboro! What in hell is Glassboro?"

Here was a director of public relations who lucked in. Before Johnson and Kosygin helped him out, he had, above all, been stuck with a name like Glassboro. It is a name with neither cadence nor conjurance—conjurance being the ability to conjure up an image of ivy-covered campus buildings and serene New England-style academic atmosphere. Then, suddenly, he was rescued from obscurity: Presto! Glassboro became associated with peace, diplomacy and two of the most powerful men in the world, David Brinkley and Walter Cronkite.

There are lessons for you to learn from this. You should get out an atlas and a ruler and start measuring. Then when you have finished your calculations, you can write the White House: "Dear Sir: Our college is exactly halfway between Washington, D.C., and Upper North Pinetree, Maine, and should the Premier of the Soviet Union ever be visiting Upper North Pinetree, we can offer excellent and equidistant facilities for any summit conference that you may have in mind."

This, however, offers only long-range prospects of success. It is difficult to plan either a public lecture series or a commencement around the possibility that a summit conference might descend upon your campus in time to get the programs printed and the mailing list informed.

The most appropriate time to get a big-name speaker on your campus is at commencement. In the first place, big namers expect to address commencements, and they are more willing at that time to be enticed to your school. Secondly, and more importantly, the process is cheap. If you invite a prominent person to the college during the academic year, he will probably demand a large lecture fee; at commencement you can substitute an honorary Litt.D. for the fee.

If you are put in charge of finding the commencement speaker, it is best to start early, since any lengthy delays may mean that all the prominent people will have been snapped up by other colleges. You will be left with either a friend of your president or the local congressman.

Just for laughs, you can ask the students whom they would like to see on campus. Their choice will be either the current idol of the student protest movement or the leading advocate of the theory that marijuana is good for you.

You can also ask the faculty for its opinion, but this is an equal waste of time. Most will urge the selection of a former professor who would read a paper in their specialty, or perhaps combine science with humanities, as in "Botany in the Time of Plato."

Finally, you can ask the president. He has the most logical choice of all—the President of the United States.

"He might come, you know," the president tells you with glaring eye. "It would depend upon the kind of letter you wrote him, of course."

If you suggest that the possiblility is remote, you will be told: "Well, he might send the Vice-President."

So the first thing you do is write the White House. Emphasize that your college is a perfect reflection of the President's views on education.

The White House will decline. It will do so politely, and with regret. Give the letter to your president. Then he can tell the board of trustees and the faculty, "We almost had the President of the United States here as our commencement speaker. Unfortunately, in a personal letter to me—I've met him, you may remember—he had to decline because of a busy schedule. But I would like to point out how this reflects our college's increased status in the country."

Be sure to leak news of the White House letter to the local newspaper. Don't do it with a formal press release, since that would look too ostentatious. If you do it quietly and with sophistication, the local paper may mention the fact in an editorial in which it agrees with your president about the increased stature of the college.

If all else fails, you can turn to the board of trustees for help in getting a speaker. The board may choose one of its own for the role, providing he gets an honorary degree. On the other hand, the members may ask one of their friends to make the speech. He probably will be the chairman of an oil company or the managing director of an investment trust. The object of this exercise is to let him see the campus, with the hope that he spots a building he would like named in his honor.

If you are extraordinarily lucky, you may get a political candidate during an election year. It would be even better if you could get a politician who would announce during the commencement address that he has decided to run for President.

This assures national publicity. You can clip the news stories of the event and send them to friends of the college, alumni, and parents. The problem, however, is that 90 per cent of the national news accounts of his speech will either spell the name of your college incorrectly or omit it altogether.

Perhaps, best of all, you can get a mention in *Newsweek*. If you do, the president is certain to stare at you scornfully and say, "I wish it had been in *Time*." In any case, the publicity will help the director of development in his efforts to boost annual giving.

8

DEVELOPMENT:

The Methodology of Making a Fat Cat Purr

Civilized nations have collapsed because they did not have a proper director of development. Nero staged what appears to have been a last-minute benefit concert in an effort to raise funds for the Rome fire department, but was too late. On the other hand, America is a great nation today, able to wage wars and reach the moon, because of the success of the countrywide annual giving campaign, which ends April 15.

When asked to explain the great moral precept that guides their intellectual philosophies, college presidents are likely to answer, "Money is the root of all success." Further, if you wind up a college president like a music box, he will sing, to the tune of your choice, "Tuition does not cover the cost of a student's education."

If you consider the appalling expenses of any college or university, you can see why tuition is insufficient. Should a student's tuition be divided up like a pie, slices would go to pay for his professors, the administrators and their secretaries, library books, and the athletic program. More slices would be needed for new brooms for the janitors and extra trash bins to handle the beer cans; for stamps used by the public relations office to mail out copies of speeches by the president; for steak dinners eaten by admissions officers while they are on the road, and for gas for the school car when it is used by the director of development for weekend fishing trips to woo a fat cat. Then, too, buildings must be paid for and test tubes bought so that the science division can carry out research projects.

It is no wonder that higher education is in such a financial bind today and why the annual giving campaign is therefore a cornerstone of our society.

As members of college boards of trustees know, money is the only factor that matters in education. This means that you have now reached the make-or-break point of your training. The question of whether you will become a college president will be answered to a large extent by your ability to raise funds.

You will not find it too difficult to become a director of development, either at your college or a neighboring institution. This is due to rapid turnover. If a director of development is doing a really superb job for his college, he is almost certain to be hired away at a higher salary by some other school down the road. If he isn't doing a good job, he is certain to be fired. This means that openings occur constantly.

You will be able to prove your ability at fund-raising by an outwardly simple yet extremely difficult test: by trying to get a personal donation from the president for some worthy charity.

Suppose the chairman of the board of trustees hears that you want to be the director of development. He calls you in for an interview, since the trustees feel it is their duty to approve the fund-raiser. "What is your experience?" the chairman asks.

"Well," you say, "last week I got fifty cents out of the president for the office coffee pool."

"My God!" the chairman exclaims. "You do have talent, don't you!"

Life will not be totally easy after that, but it is always necessary to overcome the first hurdle. You must never forget, however, that out there in the wide world are hundreds of other persons just as fearful of donating as your president. Also, there are hundreds of persons like yourself wanting someone else's money. Once you join the society of fund-raisers, you are in the company of the Internal Revenue Service, the churchmen, the Save-Our-Covered-Bridges Society, the Protect Chipmunks League, the community chesters, grocers, lawyers, mechanics, and in fact everyone you know.

Your job is to get your hand in the till before anyone else gets there. In essence, this means that your annual giving campaign must be more persuasive than that of the Protect Chipmunks League.

Start by Boosting Tuition

Before moving on to the intricacies of the Campaign, it must be pointed out that the best way for a college to raise funds is to increase tuition. To be sure, this has its strict limitations. Faculty salaries may be raised on the average of 10 per cent a year. Tuitions cannot be increased by that amount every year or not even the most wealthy would be able to send their kids to college. It is permissible, however, to jack up the cost of a college education every several years, on the assumption that even the income of the Rockefellers rises every so often.

There is a certain technique to doing this. It involves a letter to parents that must be sent out by the president. You can write the letter, but make certain the president signs it. His name has more of an aura of academic honesty.

At least five paragraphs are necessary. The first, written with pride, emphasizes the accomplishments of the college. It describes the superb value of your school's educational system to the intellectual betterment not only of the parents' child, but of all mankind.

The second paragraph, toned in sadness, points out that quality education costs money, and that tuition does not cover the cost of a student's education.

The third paragraph is brief: "Therefore, to our deep regret, the board of trustees has found it necessary to increase the cost of tuition next year by $150."

Paragraph four is quite lengthy. In great detail, it outlines the many programs of financial and scholarship aid at the college, hinting that all anyone has to do is apply and the request will be granted immediately. The implication is that the tuition increase really will cost less in the long run because there is now a staggering amount of financial aid available to students to offset it. Most parents and students will subsequently apply for aid, and will be turned down on the grounds that "others have greater need than you."

The fifth and final paragraph, couched in warm, friendly terms, cordially invites the parents to come in to see the president on their next visit to the campus. The salutation is either "Cordially" or "Very Sincerely Yours."

Parents who rebel at the tuition increase, and consider withdrawing their child to send him to another college, will find that the alternative they had in mind has just jumped its tuition by a similar amount.

Don't Woo Your Wife—Woo the Constituents

This modest boost will make only a small dent in operating expenses, so it is necessary to look elsewhere for money. The sources for funds are to be found among the various college "publics," or "constituencies"—parents again, alumni, friends of the college, local businessmen, contractors who have done work for the college, and fat cats. As director of development, you must woo these constituents with the same passion that you used to win your wife. If you value your job, it would be better to pay more attention to the constituents than to your wife; she will not give you money to run the college.

Parents represent a never-ending source of income to the college treasury. The theory is that if they have enough interest and wealth to support a son or daughter through four years of college, they have enough wealth to help support the sons and daughters of other parents who do not wish to contribute to annual giving. Once a college has grabbed a parent with money, it is reluctant to let go.

At least twice a year, the parent will receive a letter from the president asking for a "contribution to your son's education" above and beyond tuition. This will continue for each year that the son is in college. When he graduates, the parent's name will be transferred to the "former parents" list, and he will be asked to support the college that was good enough to give his son a degree. When the son gets married and raises a family and sends his children off to college, the parent will be transferred to the "grandparents" list and be asked for still more contributions.

Parents would save colleges a great deal of time and postage stamps if they would simply tithe their income to the school for the rest of their lives. Since they don't, one of your first tasks as director of development will be to find which parents have money to give away.

This is accomplished in several ways: The first is to make certain that the admissions application has a space on it calling for "father's occupation." You will have scored when you see that a freshman has written down "bank president" or "company director." Some rich children will be deliberately obscure, however, and will say that their fathers are "accountants." This could very well mean that the father is treasurer of General Motors.

In any case, your next step is to cross-check the names of parents with the bible, otherwise known as Standard & Poor's. If a parent is listed in this reference book of industry and industrialists, he is financially qualified to donate money to your college.

Parents' Day

After diligent research, you will be able to dig out the names of the wealthiest parents. Then you will be ready for action on Parents' Day. This should be held in the fall, since new students are still somewhat idealistic then and have not yet written home to complain about the crummy college they are being forced to attend.

For the success of your mission, it is important that a central registration desk be established and that parents be told they are to sign in there and be given name tags. You or an assistant can then stand by the registration desk and pick out the parents who are listed in Standard & Poor's. When you have them all identified, you must inform the president and point them out to him. He will immediately break off the conversation he has been having with the parents of a student who is on full scholarship.

The president should spend the rest of the morning charming the wealthy parents, pointing out the beauties of the school, discussing the Goal of Excellence, and slipping in little reminders that tuition does not cover the cost of a student's education.

If the father is not only listed in Standard & Poor's but has a chunk about himself in Who's Who, and is connected with some foundation, the president must take the whole family to dinner. It is best in these circumstances if the president chooses a nearby inn or hotel for eating. Nothing can destroy financial Identity faster than cold chicken à la king in the college dining hall.

When the president has completed his pitch, have him turn the father over to you. Then you must make an appointment on the spot to see Dad at his office to discuss "further points about the college that might interest you." Never mind if his office is in a city 400 miles away. Go there anyhow: parents do not like to be solicited on campus. Furthermore, they are not likely to have their checkbooks with them on such occasions, and the most you can hope for is some loose change.

Fathers do expect to be touched for money at their offices. The secretaries that you must pass to get to them, the thick rug on the floor, and the fake mahogany paneling on the walls give fathers a feeling of security. They believe this armor will frighten you and lessen your chances of talking them into a donation larger than they want to afford.

This means that you should be constantly on the offensive. If you are, the conversation might go this way:

"Good afternoon. You're the fellow from my son's college. I remember your face now. Saw you after that ghastly lunch at the inn with your president."

"Yes, sir. It's too bad about the inn. You should have eaten in the college dining hall. We really have a first-class chef."

"My son says the food there is hideous."

"We do the best we can with the money we have. You certainly wouldn't want us to take away money from your son's academic program and put it into food, would you?"

"Hardly. But with the appalling tuition you people charge, I don't see why you can't do both."

"I'm afraid that tuition doesn't cover the cost of a student's education."

"Your president mentioned that. Often. Over and over again."

"But it's true. You can't have quality without spending money. You, of all people, should know that. Your company produces the best shoes in America, and you have to spend money on that kind of quality."

"Oh, you like our shoes, do you?"

"Wear them constantly. Have five pairs at home."

"Good for you. We're quite proud of our product. Now, what did you say I can do for you?"

"I would like to discuss the tax advantages that come from giving financial donations to higher education. Specifically, to your son's college."

"I know all about tax advantages or I wouldn't have let you come see me. How much do you want?"

"For five thousand dollars, you could help us hire a new professor for political science. Your son takes political science, doesn't he?"

"I wouldn't give you five thousand unless you named the student union in my honor."

"That's out of the question. It's ridiculously cheap for a building that size. Would you settle for a reading room in the library? We've got a nice one that hasn't been named yet."

"I'll do it for twenty-five hundred."

"Three thousand?"

"Three thousand only if I get a season's football ticket and my son gets a private room in the dormitory."

"Three thousand with the free ticket only. The private room costs another four hundred."

"Okay, three thousand even. You've got yourself a deal, Mister."

If this parent seems interested in the college for the sake of education in America as well as for a tax deduction, you must try to get him on the parents' annual giving committee. Then, letters of solicitation to other parents can go out under his letterhead and over his signature. This makes giving money more chummy than if you, an official of the college, made the appeal. You can explain that no actual work is involved since you will write the letter and pay the postage.

Ethics Doesn't Pay for Buildings

As a newcomer to this game, the ethics of the maneuvering may bother you. These qualms will quickly disappear once you become a professional fund-raiser. Ethics doesn't pay for a building.

As one fund-raiser wrote in "Techniques," a publication of the American College Public Relations Association, "In discussing the solicitation of parents, and the cold, calculated organizing which takes place, it is easy to think that all is superficial, false, and that we are really not interested in parents or students other than what we can get out of them. We must be interested in raising funds, and it is natural to select those publics which have the greatest interest. Thus we make no apologies for organizing and soliciting parents for the support of higher education in America."

Once the parents' annual giving campaign is underway, checks will start rolling in. You must keep a daily tally of these, not for bookkeeping purposes, but in order to remind the president that you are doing your job. The president, in turn, will want the figures so that he can show the board of trustees that he is doing his job.

You should also work up a careful form letter to acknowledge, with thanks, each check as it comes in. If the contributions are large enough, you can stick in a paragraph that says something nice about the parents' son or daughter. This demonstrates your personal concern.

Unfortunately, some of the sons or daughters will have just been summoned to the dean of students' office on marijuana charges, or else will have been haled before the academic dean as a result of flunking four mid-term examinations. In these cases you can write, "Johnny is fitting in with his classmates."

Perhaps you will telephone the dean of students for a recommendation, and he will say that Johnny is the head of a gang that has been terrorizing the girls' dormitory. Now you can say, "Johnny is showing real leadership qualities."

The letter you always hope to write declares proudly, "Johnny, I am happy to say, is on the Dean's Honors List for this semester and is a candidate for one of the offices of Student Government, and we are very happy to have him as one of our students." This means that the college has not only done what it should for Johnny, as the admissions office had promised, but that you have a contented set of parents on the contribution rolls.

Trying to Shame the Alumni

Another large and occasionally wealthy constituency are the alumni. The old grads are an easier mark than parents, largely because of Identification. Parents identify with an institution in the sense that it is the place that is costing them $15,000 in tuition, room, board and incidentals over a four-year period.

Alumni, however, identify with the college as the place where they got a degree and an education. They do not identify with giving money to it, because their mothers and fathers spent the $15,000.

It is only in their senior year, just prior to graduation, that students make a financial contribution to the college. This is when they must pay a share of the senior class gift. The per-student share of the class gift averages out to seventy-five cents a person. A feeling of guilt is produced which carries over into later years and is one reason why alumni contributions are fairly large.

Shocking as it may appear to your president, it is not enough to send a simple letter to alumni asking for money. Many presidents cannot understand this, and insist that a mailing go out to all graduates saying, "It is about time you contributed to your college."

Alums, even those who have graduated from Harvard or Sarah Lawrence, are no different from the rest of us and must be enticed to part with a check. Some of the same techniques that apply to parents can be used here—including having an alumni association with a graduate at its head who writes letters urging members to help the common cause. It is imperative, however, that you yourself write this fund-raising letter, since the alum will be weak on spelling and grammar. This is particularly true if he is a graduate of the humanities, the science or social studies division, or of the school of agriculture, music, or medicine.

One tested letter technique involves trying to shame the alumni into parting with a contribution. An appeal can go out over the signature of the chairman of the agricultural school alumni association in which he tells his fellow farmers the dire news: "The School of Theater Alumni Association has topped our contributions by 75 per cent. I urge you to get Agriculture right back on top!"

Not wanting to let a bunch of fairies get so much credit, the farmers send in their donations. Next year, the school of theater, which is now behind agriculture in contributions, uses a similar approach to its members.

It also is necessary to have an alumni publication that is sent out three or four times a year. The alumni newsletter serves as a reminder to graduates that the college played a big role in their lives and will continue to do so. The alumni newsletter tracks down the graduate wherever he goes. He cannot get rid of it even if he moves to Tibet, so he might as well surrender and send in a check.

You will have no trouble in creating a format for the newsletter. It is simplicity itself. The first page contains a series of articles on the new buildings that are being planned for the campus, with a breakdown of costs. The second page has a lengthy editorial from the director of alumni affairs, plus a Letter from the President which the director has also written. These point out that the new buildings can be put up only with the aid of substantial contributions from alumni, who owe the money because the college gave them a proud academic heritage.

Page three contains a description of the faculty members who have just been hired. This is accompanied by an interview with the academic dean, who says with pride that each professor is an outstanding scholar who will do credit to the college. The dean also emphasizes that the college has had to pay a great deal of money for these professors and is counting on the support of its alumni to help defray the costs of maintaining a highly qualified faculty.

On the back page is a list of alumni, grouped by graduation year, with brief descriptions of the positions they now hold in industry, plus notices of new additions to their families. The purpose is to keep the alumni informed of the doings and whereabouts of their old classmates. It also permits the director of development to discover which alumni are in high-paying jobs.

One day you will notice that a graduate has just been appointed vice president and treasurer of a major corporation. You must immediately write him a letter asking for an appointment.

He writes back, not only agreeing to see you but inviting you to dinner at his club, which you have dreamed of seeing ever since it was written up in Playboy. You inform the president of the nature of your trip. He gets quite excited and reminds you, "We still have not named that new dormitory, you know."

Armed with brochures and photographs, all written and taken since the alum's graduation to show how the college has matured with the times, you fly off to see him. The meeting is an enormous success. Before you even start the pitch, he disarms you with the comment, "I know why you are here, and I want to say that I am more than willing to make a contribution." After a marvelous dinner, you fly back home confident that you will get a check large enough to make the president and the board of trustees very happy.

Two days later, it arrives. The check is for $5.00, and a note is attached: "Because of the uncertainty of business conditions, I am unable to do more at this time."

Planning THE Campaign

Your most immediate necessity is to go elsewhere to find the money that will offset the $500 spent on this last abortive trip. The president will remind you acidly that you need at least $495.

Now is the time to plan the Campaign in detail. Successful fund-raising involves 95 per cent planning and 5 per cent collecting. You must set a monetary goal, and find a project that this money will finance. When you have laid this foundation, you can start soliciting your constituents, whether they be alumni, parents, or friends of the college.

One group of constituents will be the owners of the firms that have done business with the college. Most colleges operate on the theory that any contractor who does work for the institution should, in return, donate a portion of his bill to annual giving. This is a marvelous philosophy. There are many who wish it would carry over into everyday life. Thus you would invite a plumber to your house to fix a leaky faucet, and, when he subsequently sends you a bill for $100, you pay him. At the end of the year, you call on the plumber and point out that since you gave him $100 worth of business during the year, it is not only his duty but his privilege to refund 10 per cent of it as a Christmas gift.

Gluggle Hall

Contractors and plumbers aside, however, your most important constituent is the fat cat. As his prime prerequisite for the role, a fat cat must have money that he is willing to share with you. Not *able* to share, but willing. Unfortunately, few people are willing to share their money with anyone other than themselves and their immediate family. It is your job to convince the fat cat that he should Identify with your college. In this respect, you are helped enormously by the Internal Revenue Service's gentle eyes when it comes to contributions to higher education made either by a fat cat or a plumber.

You also are helped by the fact that you have buildings to be named and are in a position to trade a lasting memorial for a hefty check. It is an odd but proven fact that many of the fat cats will have names such as "Gluggle." No doubt you will have qualms about Gluggle Hall being named Gluggle Hall, but look upon it as a necessary part of fulfilling the purpose of higher education to create a better society for all.

Many and devious are the ways to approach fat cats with the aim of materializing Gluggle Hall out of their wallets—or if not Gluggle Hall, at least ten laboratories in the science building. Don't bother with fat cats if all the president wants is a new shelf for the library. You can get that from a contractor or a parent; it's minuscule. Save the fat cats for the big splurge.

The first rule for fat cats is to find a project that they will be willing to finance. It should, above all, be important not only to the success of your college, but to the satisfaction of the donor's ego. This being the case, a new sewer system simply will not do. Every college has a sewer problem, based on the inexorable rule that the more students there are, the greater the cumulative need to dispose. No one, not even a Rockefeller, wants his name attached to a sewage-disposal plant.

On the other hand, a new dormitory will do nicely. You can get one housing approximately one hundred students for around $400,000. The trouble with dormitories, however, is that the Department of Housing and Urban Development, whose expenditures are funded by the United States Congress, has a fine dormitory-financing program available. You would be an idiot not to have your college take advantage of it. Ignore projects that the taxpayer will finance anyway.

Science buildings, field houses and libraries are ideal for fat cats. You can also have one of them endow a Chair, thus taking a faculty member's salary out of the college's operating expenses and putting it in the fat cat's billfold.

A field house is a particularly nice fat cat Identity project. The Federal Government will not provide financing for a field house if it is to be used solely for intercollegiate sports, and this, of course, is *why* the president and the coaches want a field house.

You must be aware, however, that your college may not be able to pay the money needed to attract good athletes. In that case, the president may decide in the future—after his teams have been trounced by everyone including the local high school, and he has fired four coaches on the grounds it *must* be their fault—that the college should concentrate instead on "academics." This sounds idealistic; he does not want to sink into the gutter of big-time athletics. In fact, it is merely an excuse to get out from under a losing proposition that made the alumni unhappy. Therefore, be sure that your college can buy an athletic team before pressing a fat cat into erecting a field house.

The Fat-Cat Dinner

Whatever the project, it must benefit your individual college. When you have decided on it, you must start wooing fat cats. If there are several such cats in your area, try throwing a fat-cat dinner.

First, consult with the president and your fellow administrators on whom to invite. This is not too hard, since sooner or later the name of every rich man and woman in the community will have come to the college's attention. A good director of development is one who latches onto every snatch of gossip that he can find about the constituency. Joe So-and-So gave $10,000 to the community chest, and Albert Whozis has two Cadillacs—or one Cadillac and a seven-horsepower snow-blower—and so on.

Wording of invitations is crucial. Never let on that you are holding a candlelight and sonata seduction dinner for the express purpose of raising money. If you do, no one will come. Instead, invite the fat cats to "tour the college" or "see the new library collection" or "meet our distinguished new faculty members."

Mark the invitations RSVP. Then you can get a fairly accurate estimate of how many are coming, and thus approximate the magnitude of the dinner. The stomachs of students throughout the nation are lined with food left over from the previous night's fat-cat feast, when the kitchen was told to prepare dinner for 96 and only 14 showed up. This costs *you* money, not the students. It also raises dangerous questions in the minds of students as to why they can't eat that well every day.

The choice of food for the type of dinner under discussion is a delicate subject. Fried chicken is out because that is farm food, and you are trying to raise money, not alfalfa. Ignore the fact that nearly everyone loves fried chicken. It is appearance, not taste, that counts, and fried chicken is low on the scale of appearance. It looks too common.

Never serve liver.

Good cuts of steak also are out, because the cost of good steak is so high that you would need a separate fund drive just to raise dinner money.

What you really want is a steamship round of roast beef. On the appearance scale, this rates an A, particularly when there is a chef in a tall white hat doing the carving. The fact that steamship round is nothing but roasted round steak, and therefore often tough, is more or less beside the point, particularly if you have planned the pre-dinner drinking festivities to perfection.

Drinks are a necessity, both to keep up your courage and to lighten the atmosphere. Furthermore, the alcoholic content of a fat-cat dinner is often crucial to its success. A sober fat cat will listen sullenly to your pitch after dinner and then get up and go home. One who is just properly drunk will applaud everything you say. The man who has had one too many will jump to his feet and yell, "God damn this lousy college anyway." Or else he will pass out during dessert and never learn why he should Identify with the college.

Some of the best bartenders in the world are students, specifically those who come from well-to-do families. They learned how to mix the perfect martini before they graduated from high school. Do not, therefore, be hesitant about hiring a group of students to serve drinks. If you explain the challenge of getting just the right degree of alcohol into a fat cat, the students will rise to the occasion and exert more effort than they would on a term paper. This is also the case if you give them the incentive of free beer and all the gossip they can carry back to the dormitory.

It's Time for Your Speech

Once dinner is finished and coffee and dessert have been served, it is time for your speech. This is known as "the pitching hour" and everyone in the audience has been dreading it. Finish your coffee, wipe your chin carefully since grease does not go well with fund-raising, and go to the podium. Hardly anyone in the audience will look back at you, but don't be embarrassed; they know you are going to make a speech and are postponing the pain as long as possible.

The opening line is crucial. Do not improvise. Play it safe. If you look serious and declare, "I am delighted to see you all tonight," you simply cannot go wrong.

Most of your audience is now wondering why they have been invited. Build the suspense, like Agatha Christie. Drop clues en route. Emphasize that you have invited all these friends out in front to sup at your table because you want to tell them what the college can do for their community—*their* community, not "the" community; not what they can do for you, but what you can do for them.

At this point, of course, you must have well in mind what exactly it is that you can do for them. It is best to use the culture approach. Talk about the influence of the lecture series on the community, and provide a schedule of all the concerts that the music department is offering free to the public.

Talk about the quality of the faculty, and how nice it is for the community to have all these brilliant men living in their neighborhood.

Unless you cannot avoid it, do not mention students. Undoubtedly most of those in the audience have been horrified by the shaggies around town, and they may have told each other that beatniks and peaceniks and nutniks and flower people were taking over the community, and that this is a bad thing. It is a known fact among colleges that the only students who ever are noticed by townspeople are the shaggies. The clean ones and the bright ones, who are in the majority, are dismissed as visitors or else ignored.

It is possible that you can mention some particular service of the student body to the community, such as all the corpuscles they poured into the blood-donor drive. However, you'd do well to hope that when the students told you they were going to participate in a blood-donor drive, they were not thinking of giving it to the Viet Cong or whomever else the United States happens to be fighting at the time.

At any rate, get this portion of the speech out of the way and begin dropping hints about money. Introduce this aspect gently. The best way is to emphasize quality education. Define quality: a good deodorant costs money, but it protects you in a crowd; good education costs money, but it protects your society—that kind of thing.

Make certain that you have a few statistics about the college available. One set might consist of the number of volumes in the library and the cost thereof, and how many more are needed; another might be the number of rock samples that you had to buy for geology. "Why, we even had to get a monkey's skull for the biology people," you can add, properly astonished.

By this time the fat cats will be aware, if they had not caught on before, that (a) colleges need money, and (b) their money is what you had in mind.

Start now to brush the picture with a light stroke; there will be plenty of time later to slap paint in their faces. All you have done at the dinner is to lay the foundation for an approach to them individually later on. End up with a joke, say "I thank you all for coming," and sit down. Applause will follow, and the dinner will break up. Most of those present will head quickly for the door. If you have been persuasive, one of the fat cats will come up to you and shake your hand and congratulate you on the marvelous and inspiring talk, which provided insights into the needs of colleges that he had not seen before.

Jump to your feet and shake his hand and point out that you have been meaning to come around to his office to talk about the college. Make an appointment on the spot. Whatever you do, don't forget to address him by name, particularly if it is Gluggle.

Get a Geriatrician on the Board of Trustees

If you do not find a willing fat cat at this dinner, you are almost certain to be given the name of another by a member of the board of trustees. The function of the board of trustees is to name buildings, fire the president if the college is going bankrupt, issue stern warnings against student demonstrations, and raise money. The director of development is most interested in this latter category. Therefore it is in your interest to see that a geriatrician is named to the board.

Since the geriatrician's patients are the very elderly, they are candidates for deferred giving. Medical ethics will prevent the physician from telling you which of his rich patients is about to depart for heavenly pastures. However, he may show up late to a trustee's meeting complaining that he has been up all night attending to Mr. Well Thee, who doesn't have long to go.

You should immediately collect all your charts showing estate tax benefits from gifts to higher education, and rush off to see Mr. Thee's lawyer or perhaps the big man himself. The pitch is the standard you-can't-take-it-with-you approach, coupled with strong emphasis on the fact that if he makes a provision in his will for the college, the Internal Revenue Service won't get all his money. To close the deal, you can point out that his name will be seen by far more people on the new science building than it will on a tombstone.

Perhaps Mr. Thee will ignore you and die without attending to deferred giving, in which case the Internal Revenue Service will collect a great deal of money for the Government's coffers. He also may ignore both you and the Government and put his money into a foundation.

Now it is your responsibility to get your share of Mr. Thee's money out of the Government or the foundation.

First you call a conference of the president, the academic dean, and the chairman of the science division to see what project they can think of that the Government or a foundation would finance. It is a waste of time to bring in someone from humanities. No one wants to give money to humanities.

The Ideal Project for Government Support

The Government is one of the best sources of money, since its primary aim is to help all education while helping itself and the rest of the country. National Defense, Oppressed Minorities, and Social Problems that affect the

Majority must be stressed in any application to the Government. A perfect request, then, would be headed: "The Effect of Air Pollution on the Navajo Indians, as It Concerns National Defense and the Easing of Racial Tensions in Big Cities, with Beneficial Consequences to the Gross National Product."

No congressman will get angry at that. Furthermore, you will have put the students on the spot. If they threaten to demonstrate against National Defense and the Gross National Product, they will be in the position of supporting air pollution and opposing Navajo Indians and slum dwellers.

Obscurity also helps. Scientists and the government never know when some obscure fact may turn up that will revolutionize thinking and Ph.D. theses. You may be able to get a federal grant to pay for a year's sabbatical for a professor if you submit a proposal for "A Census of Trees in the Gobi Desert."

The foundations also are a source of funds, but their prime requirement for giving away money is that you be famous. Perhaps you need only $200,000 to overhaul your academic program and make it among the best of small colleges in the country. Don't bother to apply to the large foundations. They are too busy donating $5 million to Yale.

One final note about being a director of development: Do not stay in the job too long if you are a sociable person who likes to have friends. Sooner or later, your friends will stop seeing you. It is too uncomfortable for them to talk while at the same time clutching their wallets.

9

ANATOMY OF A RIOT

When you have reached this point, you should have mastered the fundamental techniques involved in administering a college. It is time, therefore, to move on to the top and become a college president. Before doing so, it is best to have a review of administrative functions.

No better way presents itself for this than to discuss what happens in a riot. All of your talents will be called upon to handle the various facets of a student uprising.

The one person certain to lose as a result of a riot is the president. He may not be fired right away, but he may suffer such indignities that he will be leery of showing up to deliver the commencement address.

The author is fortunate to have had placed in his hands various documents relating to a college riot. They are presented here for your edification. It is to be hoped that you can take advantage of the lessons taught herein and

knock the remaining obstacle to the furtherance of your
career off the ladder and onto the ground.

EXCERPTS FROM THE REPORT OF HENRY BLOOD, JR.,
CHAIRMAN OF THE STUDENT PEACEFUL MEANS COMMIT-
TEE, TO HIS STAFF:

"So far everything has gone according to plan. At the
present time we are occupying the Dean of Students' office
and are keeping him prisoner. He has argued that there are
only fifty of us, and that we are preventing one thousand
other students from attending class or getting an education.
Naturally we dismissed this as Establishment nonsense, and
pointed out that neither he nor the rest of the clods we
have for a student body understand the revolution which
we all are trying to lead. It takes only a few to guide the
many. I told him this was the essence of participatory
democracy. He disagreed completely, and I had to hit him
several times to change his mind."

EXCERPTS FROM THE LETTER OF MRS. HENRY BLOOD,
SR., TO HER SON:

"Darling—

"Your father and I were shocked to see you on television. It was very embarrassing for us to see your beard.
This caused many awful comments from our friends at
the Club, and we had to go home early. I really don't
understand what you are trying to accomplish, and neither
does your father. The news really ruined his day, which
was such a shame. He broke 90 on the Club course, and
you know how hard that course is, and he was so happy
until he came into the bar and saw you on television. Did I

write you that we have bought a new car? It is a Cadillac, of course, but this one is blue. You will love to drive it when you get home."

TEXT OF A LETTER FROM I.G. LOO, A STUDENT AT THE COLLEGE, TO HIS PARENTS:
"Dear Folks:

"It is very warm in this part of the world. I miss home often, particularly the tundra. The students are very nice. They say I am an oppressed minority, and they feel very guilty that we have no course here at the college on Eskimo literature. They are staging a protest and hope to get the faculty to start teaching Eskimo literature. I have told them this is tokenism, but they are going ahead anyway. Do we have any literature? There is a group of students here on campus who are very angry. They want all the dormitories to be segregated so that the whites can live with the whites and the blacks with the blacks. They say that any other way is genocide. I am the only Eskimo on campus, and if this plan is adopted I am afraid I will be very lonely living by myself."

A MEMO FROM THE DEAN OF STUDENTS TO THE PRESIDENT:
"After long and painful talks with the Student Peaceful Means Committee, I have extracted from them their conditions for ending the revolt. They are listed in priority:

"1. Unlimited and unquestioned distribution of The Pill to all women asking for it.

"2. Abolition of all visitation restrictions in the dormitories, both men's and women's. An end to the Proctor system so that there will be no supervision in the dormitories.

"3. Substitution of the pass/fail system for the grades system.

"4. An end to the practice of taking attendance in class.

"5. Student participation in faculty meetings and curriculum meetings, with the students having the right to veto courses which they oppose.

"6. Abolition of the science requirement.

"7. Abolition of the social studies requirement.

"8. Abolition of the humanities requirement.

"9. The students are to have the sole right to say whether or not faculty members should be hired or rehired.

"10. Certain members of the administration may keep their jobs, but their function will be to supervise the maintenance department."

MEMO FROM AN ENGLISH PROFESSOR TO THE ACADEMIC DEAN:

"I have studied the students' demands, and may I be permitted to say that most of the list is legitimate. Grades are only an artificial measure of a student's capability, and perhaps the grade system only encourages meaningless cramming rather than real learning. I agree with the pass/fail system.

"Furthermore, I believe that the students should be represented at the meetings of the faculty and the curriculum committees. It is, after all, their education that concerns us, and they should have a right to voice their views.

"There is much to be said for the abolition of the science and social studies requirements. Requirements only restrict creativity. I feel confident in my own mind that they will have second thoughts on humanities, which are, after all, the essence of a liberal arts education. Certainly science has been overemphasized in our time.

"There has been a lack of control over maintenance, as I am sure you have noticed. Incidentally, I am out of chalk."

MEMO FROM THE CHAIRMAN OF THE SCIENCE DIVISION TO THE ACADEMIC DEAN:

"Abolish the science requirement? They are out of their God-damn' minds!"

A NEWS RELEASE FROM THE PUBLIC RELATIONS OFFICE:

"The President of the college issued the following statement today:

"'The news media have distorted the significance of the small so-called demonstration on our campus, led by an equally small number of students. We are studying their alleged demands, but we wish to emphasize that nothing can be achieved by violence. Whether the demands are legitimate or not is beside the point in the current atmosphere. The news media could perform a greater service to the public by emphasizing the positive accomplishments of this college and its faculty and student body.'"

EXCERPT FROM THE TELEVISION NEWS THAT EVENING:

"The president of the local college hinted today that the demands of the thousands of student demonstrators on his campus are legitimate. This was the interpretation by informed academic circles of his remark, and I quote, 'whether the demands are legitimate or not. . . .' More news after this important message about your dishpan hands."

SHOUT OF RELIEF FROM HENRY BLOOD, JR., TO HIS FELLOW CONSPIRATORS IN THE DEAN OF STUDENTS' OFFICE:
"Hey, did you hear that? We've won!"

MEMO FROM THE DIRECTOR OF DEVELOPMENT TO THE PRESIDENT:
"The lawyer for Mr. Well Thee just called and said his client is going to withdraw his deferred giving bequest unless we get this campus calmed down and get rid of the communist agitators."

INSTRUCTION FROM THE PRESIDENT TO HIS SECRETARY:
"Get me the police on the telephone."

10

THE PUSH TO THE TOP RUNG:

How to Make Like, Not War

The police will respond to the president's summons with enthusiasm, and the students will be equally delighted to see them. Students battle the Establishment by taunting and kicking cops; cops battle the Establishment by slugging students. If it were not for aching heads and bruised flesh, these encounters could be therapeutic for both sides.

Since gladiators do get hurt, it is best to refrain from calling in the police when there is trouble on campus. It not only will cause the revolt to spread from the original fifty to all one thousand of their classmates, but will lead to such a run on bandages at the college infirmary that you will have to set aside a portion of annual giving for re-stocking supplies.

Unfortunately, the terrified president has not learned this lesson and will order police to quell a riot. When he does, his term of office will have started to end. The board of trustees must find a scapegoat for the ensuing unfavorable publicity, and the president is the only logical choice. He represents Authority, which the students distrust and which caused them to riot in the first place. When trouble does occur, he then represents *lack* of Authority, because he was unable to prevent a breakdown in law and order. Hemmed in on all sides, he has to go.

Convince Them You Have a Plan

Given the times we live in, it can be said with certainty that protests of some sort will break out on any college campus. This is where you enter the picture. Trustees search longingly for a president who will prevent trouble. You must convince them that you have a plan for riot avoidance that will ensure lasting campus tranquility.

The first priority is to get student representation in college decisions, particularly those involving academic matters. Faculty members have resisted this for years. They have argued that students do not have the maturity or the experience to guide their own education. In addition, they have maintained that students during a given year will think only of the immediate future and will ignore long-range planning and educational goals.

For example, a group of Student Powerites would de-emphasize science because it has not led to human perfection, and would push instead for humanities and urban-affairs courses. In another year, a group would decide that only science could save the world, and out would go humanities. Professors have declared that such lack of long-range planning would create difficulties for everyone.

These faculty arguments miss the point, which is that students will make unpleasant scenes until they have their own way.

Therefore you must insist that students be represented at faculty meetings, with full voting rights. The students will be elated. They will select one or two of their number to attend faculty meetings and fight for student rights. After spending three hours listening to the professors argue violently about minutiae, the representatives will leave and never show up again. If they do continue to attend out of duty to their consciences, they probably will sleep throughout the whole session and may have to be banished because their snores prevent Modern Languages from doing his crossword puzzle.

Should this happen, it would not be your problem. You have made the gesture, which is all that counts.

Next, inform the students that you will place the biggest administrative responsibility of any college in their hands. This is parking regulations. All students know that the president spends as much time trying to find parking places for faculty members and seniors as he does fundraising, and they will be pleased that you want to entrust them with a problem of such overriding importance to the success of their education.

Their first act will be to abolish every parking regulation, invoking the principle of participatory democracy. In other words, first come, first served. This will lead to such a chaos of traffic snarls that they will have to rescind it immediately.

Next, they will forbid all freshmen and sophomores from parking in the choice spots near the campus. An uprising will ensue immediately among the lowerclassmen, but it will be directed against the student parking committee and not at the administration.

Most of the hard-core student rebels will be on this parking committee, since they will have wanted to show everyone that they can cope with authority once it is placed in their hands. After a semester of trying to achieve a solution, they will be exhausted. Furthermore, they will have spent so much time on parking that they will not have had time to study, and so will flunk out. This will rid you of the troublemakers. The students who are left on campus will hand the problem back to you, gratefully, and resume their studies.

Take Care of the Faculty

After you have dealt with student ambitions, you should turn your attention to the faculty. The problem at many colleges is that the faculty is so strong that it tells the president what to do. The great and entrenched department chairmen, secure in their tenure and their fiefdoms, act like medieval barons, each warring with the other over the potential spoils from annual giving and foundation grants. They treat the president as a symbol, impotent but necessary.

The advantage in a small and somewhat new college is that this state of affairs, though started, has not yet become full-blown. It is your task to prevent it.

Faculty members, whether they have too much power or too little, are convinced that they know more than the administration about how to run a college. To win faculty members to your side when the showdown comes on the choice of the next president, you must promise them a bigger voice in college administration.

Suppose one professor is appointed as faculty representative to the public relations office. Many professors pride themselves on being excellent photographers. The representative will insist that he be allowed to take the pictures for the new catalogue so that the unflattering and unrepresentative ones now in it can be discarded.

He will show his prints to his colleagues on the faculty. Their universal reaction will be horror. "Are you going to put that underexposed thing in the catalogue?" Or, "How come you took so many pictures of the science building?" Or, "Those aren't bad, but if you had only asked me, I could have helped you."

A bit shaken, he will ask the director of public relations for something else to do. The PR man will tell him to write a news release on a foundation grant that has just been awarded to a professor of zoology. "Zoology! Why should those bastards get foundation grants? I'll be damned if I'll write anything about zoology."

After a short while, he will go back to teaching.

The same process can be repeated in other administrative posts. A professor who has complained for years that the director of development does not know how to raise money will be appalled at the time and effort that goes into getting that $5.00 contribution from a rich alumnus. Perhaps the professor will have told his friends that the neighborhood fat cat will give a huge sum of money to the college if he is only asked. Accordingly, the director of development will happily send the professor out to solicit from the fat cat, and the fat cat will sick his Great Dane on him, and the professor will discover why so many directors of development have patches on the seats of their pants.

Finally, another professor will join the admissions office. He will insist that only those prospects with high academic scores be admitted to the college. At the end of the year, only four students will have been enrolled, and the professor will find that his classroom job is redundant.

This professor and others soon will be fleeing to the sanctuary of the faculty dining room, leaving administration up to the administration.

There is one other step you can take. From the professorial viewpoint, happiness is a reduced teaching load, preferably from twelve hours to two. You must be wary of promising this, however, despite its apparent attractions. If you reduce everyone's teaching load, you must hire more faculty members to take up the slack. The minute you start talking about expenditures, you will run into trouble with the board of trustees.

What you can do is promise faculty members that they do not have to concentrate on teaching. In an era of student unrest, some presidents will insist that their professors actually "teach"—that is, communicate knowledge—rather than just read five-year-old lecture notes or drone through a textbook. Teaching is difficult for many faculty members who find the process of communicating both unintellectual and beneath their dignity. If you assure them that they will not have to communicate, you will receive their backing for your candidacy.

Seduce the Board of Trustees

When you have won the faculty and student body to your side, you must set out to seduce the board of trustees. It is more than likely that in their search for a new president they have formed a three-man selection committee which has found some names and presented them to the full board for a decision.

Your name, incidentally, was not at the head of the list. Top billing had been given to the defeated presidential candidate in the last election, who up until then had been Vice President of the United States. The trustees felt that he had had sufficient public exposure to insure them of national publicity. They also hoped that many of the 25 million Americans who had voted for him in the election would listen sympathetically if he urged all of them to contribute to annual giving.

An offer had been quickly dispatched. A form letter from an aide had duly arrived back at the college, with its name misspelled, thanking the board for its flattering offer but adding that the candidate had made no commitments for the future. There was a don't-call-us-we'll-call-you aura which forced the trustees to look elsewhere.

The selection committee had agreed to consider your credentials because its members had heard that you were popular with both the students and the faculty. Until recently, this was not a requirement for president of a college. Now it is, because the opinion is that students and faculty members will not turn on a man who is their friend. This is not so much an opinion as it is a desperate hope.

Do You Look Like a College President?

Having satisfied themselves that you are popular with the masses, the selection committee next will take a long, hard glimpse at another important facet of your character—do you look like a college president? Image is not only extraordinarily important, but constantly changing. In the old days of Nicholas Murray Butler, it was necessary for a president to appear wise, whether he was or not. The Mr.-Chips-off-the-old-block image has been displaced.

A wise old man can discuss Cicero for hours, but he cannot necessarily raise funds from a businessman who knows that Cicero is a Chicago suburb not far from where he buys his computers. Boards of trustees would appreciate having a wise old man around as an antiquarian addition to the college's corporate image. He would add a bit of quality to modern architecture, but he must either be president emeritus or a beloved and retired professor of the humanities.

What trustees seek now is a man who is dynamic, who can be at home on a golf course with a fat cat, and who can talk on equal terms with businessmen, influential government bureaucrats, and middle-aged alumni who have made their pile.

This means that physically you may be thin, slender, stocky, or stout, but not unbecomingly fat. Consult your doctor on the safest way to reduce if you think corpulence may interfere with your presidential image. You should also have streaks of executive gray in your hair. If you don't, a few carefully placed daubs of silver model-airplane paint will help out.

It is best not to have either a beard or a mustache, although this might endear you to the shaggies. A beard sets up automatic warning signals in the minds of parents and businessmen, and a mustache makes you look more like Hitler than a college president.

You can give the impression that you are dynamic simply by moving quickly when you are around a trustee. Snap out orders to your secretary, preferably such commands as "Get me the Ford Foundation on the phone right now!" Be somewhat twitchy in the trustee's presence, as if you were granting him a favor by talking to him when you should be busy raising funds—a job which, you hint, you can do better than anyone he has known, including the Director of Internal Revenue.

Show him, as well as any prospective donor, that you are intimately acquainted with the Dow Jones Industrial Average, the movement of blue chips, and such terms as "cash flow" and "accounts receivable." Cash flow has a nice ring to it; businessmen love to spend hours talking about cash flow.

Above all, give the trustees the impression that you will not permit faculty members to spend all they want on educational instruction.

You've Got to Be Scholarly, and Religious, Too

By now, you should have passed two major tests—an ability to get along with your college constituency, and an appearance conducive to fund-raising. Unfortunately, another obstacle remains. Trustees prefer, when the showdown of selection comes, to have a president who is not only a peacemaker and a fund-raiser, but a scholar as well. This is what sets college presidents apart from other presidents, such as those of the United States, Republic Steel, and the Yum-Yum Diners, Inc. You need not fear, however, since only a short period of cramming will make up for any deficiency in your educational upbringing.

The course need take only several hours each day for three days. On the first, you can skim through Lambs' tales from Shakespeare. This will give you a quick familiarity with the plays so that, in conversation with the trustees, you'll be able to make a few allusions to Lear or Macbeth if you are talking about the burdens of office, or to Shylock if you happen to be discussing fund-raising.

On the second day, memorize large segments of Bartlett's Familiar Quotations, particularly all you can find from the Bible. This will establish you not only as a scholar but as a religious man as well. It will give you an air of dignity and contemplation to complement your dynamism.

Finally, read something that has been written by James Baldwin, not for its literary content but because he is Black. This will have the dual purpose of indicating that you understand and appreciate modern literature, and suggesting that you are familiar with the problems and aspirations of the Blacks. Therefore you must be an expert at managing a college at this particular juncture in history.

Now your credentials are intact, and all you must do is await the decision of the board of trustees. They meet on a Sunday. You are summoned to the college to hear their findings. Just before he closes the door to the meeting, the chairman of the board gives you a big wink.

The trustees stay in session for two hours, the second hour of which is devoted to a discussion of their winter vacations in Florida. When the meeting breaks up, the chairman emerges with a stranger whom he introduces as U. S. Grants, the most successful fund-raiser in the history of education. He is the new president of your college.

The chairman then puts his arm around your shoulders and says with a kindly smile, "I know you will be delighted to hear that the trustees have given you a unanimous vote of thanks for all you have done here at the college. We know you will want to stay on and assist our new president."

11

IF ALL ELSE FAILS . . . :

The Art of Being a Founding Father

An axiom of American Democracy is that any child, regardless of race, creed, color or national origin, can grow up to become president of a college. Therefore don't be discouraged, since you have started out on the same basis as everyone else in the country. By this time you also will have had experience in academic administration. This gives you an advantage over many of your fellow men, particularly those who did not go to college.

Once you have established your campus credentials, word will get around that you are presidential timber. Perhaps the new president of your school will suggest to a college he knows that you are the ideal person to be in charge. He will do this because he wants to get rid of you and bring in his own personal staff.

Other means exist of climbing to the top. One of these was discovered recently by a young administrator of a major university. He was assigned to do a study of the growing pains of two small colleges. His credentials—which combined administrative experience with a Ph.D.—impressed the presidents of both institutions. At the first college, the president told him, "We're in the market for an academic dean. Would you be interested?" At the second, the president said, "I'm moving up to become chairman of the board of trustees. Would you like to have my job?"

The administrator rejected both offers, but in the process discovered a hitherto unknown way of climbing the Ivy Ladder: if you do enough reports on small colleges, one of them will ask you to be its president.

As mentioned briefly in Chapter 1, another certain way to become a college president is to take the route of the Great War Hero, such as General Eisenhower. There also is General Mark Clark, who became president of The Citadel after an illustrious career as a combat commander. You don't have to set your sights as high as Columbia or The Citadel, since many smaller colleges are looking for war heroes to be their presidents.

The advantage of being a general is that you will be intimately acquainted with the Military/Industrial Complex, and you should be able to get profitable research contracts for your faculty. The world has a way to go yet before it finds the perfect technique for killing people. You are certain to get a sizable grant from the Complex if your students and professors can help the common cause.

The disadvantage of this route to the top is that some unfriendly soul may shoot you on the battlefield, and all of your preparations will have been wasted.

There remains one foolproof method of becoming a college president. This is to found your own college.

How to Start a College

As your first requirement, you will need a campus. Your own house will do, provided the architecture is colonial, which has more intellectual atmosphere than a suburban ranch home. Within the house you must have at least two large rooms to spare. The first is for classes and the second is for a library. A college must have a library. You can stock it with your own collection of books, which should include a good selection of 19th-century British novels and some leather-bound histories of the Roman Empire. An encyclopedia will help. Also, you should have a large dictionary, preferably one that rests on a wooden stand. All these books lend tone to a library.

Next you must seek a sufficient amount of money to get the enterprise underway. Call a few businessmen together and tell them that you are starting a new college which will be a landmark in the history of American education. Ask them to serve as trustees. Be a passionate advocate of the duty of businessmen to contribute to the public welfare by giving freely of their time and skills to higher education. It is only when they have agreed to become trustees, and have signed their names to the articles of incorporation of the new college, that you can ask them for money. Just get enough to pay for the printing of the catalogue. If you still are a bit short, then promise to name the college in honor of the businessman who will give you the biggest check. Do this only in an emergency, since it may be our old friend Gluggle or his friend Smutz. For the sake of public relations it would be better to have a more nondescript name, such as Harvard.

Once you have money in hand, get the catalogue written, printed, and ready for distribution to high school guidance counselors.

In doing this, most of your time should be spent in composing the Statement of Our Purpose in the catalogue. You should point out that in this complex, technological world, the multiversity only perpetuates grossness and evil. Emphasize that to preserve the American heritage a college should have small classes and highly individualized instruction, which you are prepared to provide.

You must declare your belief that a college education should be available to the below-average student. Describe your sympathy for these youngsters who are not equipped to fight the intellectual snobbism of the older and more prestigious institutions. This is the only kind of student you are going to get for several years, and your appeal must be directed at them from the start.

With whatever money you have left over from printing costs, you can hire a director of admissions who will carry the word to the masses. Through personal contacts with the local board of education, a few quick calls to guidance counselors at the more inadequate high schools, and the strategic placement of glowing advertisements in *The New York Times* and *The Christian Science Monitor,* he should be able to bring in at least five students.

This is a sufficiently large student body for the first year. To teach them, there is yourself, plus the director of admissions, plus the trustees. The trustees will serve without pay providing that you have put the word "Professor" in front of their names in the catalogue.

You can use the tuition money from the five students to pay the salaries of yourself and the director of admissions during the year.

You Need More than Five Students

With the first year successfully behind you, the next step is to plan for expansion. First, you contact librarians at every college in the area and ask them to give you their discards and seconds to add to your own holdings. It is not difficult to build a sizable library. Building a quality library is something else again, but this can be made the object of a fund drive in a later year.

You must also increase the size of the student body. The five students who were with you the first year undoubtedly received the highly individualized instruction that you had promised. Naturally they did not flunk out, because you could not afford to lose them. Delighted with the progress they are making toward a college diploma, they will become enthusiastic boosters and can be signed on as recruiting assistants to the director of admissions. The aim will be to bring in a total of fifty students for the second year.

Once again you invoke the principle that wherever young men or women exist, a director of admissions such as yours is ready to grab them. Therefore, you will have no trouble in filling the barn with bodies.

This means that you will have to turn over your entire

house to the college. With the big jump in tuition revenue, you will be able to rent a small apartment nearby for yourself, wife and family. With the rest of the tuition money, you can hire more faculty members. Most of these will be B.A.s, with a sprinkling of M.A.s. A Ph.D. is still out of your salary range.

Since there are no Ph.D.s on your faculty, the professors probably will be more interested in teaching and communicating knowledge than in preparing the students for admission to graduate school. Consequently, your academic fame will spread, and more students will be attracted.

Start Building

Now you are on your way and have reached the point where you can hire a director of development. His sole job at this stage is to find a fat cat who is willing to donate a large tract of land to handle the college's physical growth. Once you have the land, you must retain an architect to design the new campus. Be sure to have the architect give you a detailed drawing of his plan. This can be printed in the catalogue, giving prospective students and their parents the impression that the campus already is completed.

At the same time, you can start filling out forms for federal programs that give money to higher education. You will be able to get loans that will put the college in debt for the next hundred years, and these will enable you to get the building program underway. Don't fret about the debt, since paying it off will be the problem of succeeding generations.

If you run short of federal money for some projects, you can always use tuition revenues to put up a building. This will deprive the current student body of funds for academic programs, but don't worry about that. Simply tell the students how proud they will be when they return in five years and see the campus completed.

Now you are ready to seek formal accreditation by the regional scholastic accrediting agency. Accreditation will give you status and respectability. It also will help you to attract better students in the long run.

In general, accreditation involves the number of volumes in the library, books being a convenient measuring stick of academic excellence; the number of nice buildings on campus; the percentage of Ph.D.s on the faculty; faculty salaries, which must be high enough to keep professors from going somewhere else and thus producing teaching instability; SAT scores of the student body; financial stability, and, last and somewhat incidentally, the quality of the academic program.

To get your college ready for accreditation, you must forego any sentimentality. Remember that, to a good administrator, sentimentality only interferes with management efficiency.

First, you must fire most of the professors who have been with you since the beginning. This is because they do not have Ph.D.s The absence of doctors on the faculty will hurt your chances of getting accredited, because it shows that you have no one qualified to teach.

To replace the old guard, you must hire any Ph.D. who applies for a job. Most of the applicants will be young scholars straight out of graduate school, without much classroom experience but with a great love for obscure graduate study.

Secondly, you must insure that the nice, hard-working but not very bright students who have composed your college's student body must be flunked out or graduated as quickly as possible. Their SAT scores are too low for accreditation. To fill up their places, you must instruct the director of admissions to recruit students with much higher scores. The ones he gets will, for the most part, be poorly motivated or will have severe emotional problems. They cannot get into other colleges, so will be glad at the chance of coming to yours. The accrediting agency will be concerned only with their high SAT scores, not with their potentiality for the psychiatrist's couch.

At this point, you are ready to invite the accreditation agency to your campus. Its representatives will look it over, scowl at some things and beam at others, and pronounce their approval. You will be able to say with pride that your college is now a major force in American education.

After you have done all this, you can finally relax and enjoy your career as a benevolent college president.

By this time, however, the trustees will have become so entranced with their new toy that they will be demanding bigger buildings and more paying customers; the various divisions of the faculty will be at war with one another over who should get the most money for sabbaticals and equipment; the students will be arguing that they do not have enough participatory democracy. All will single you out as the source of their frustrations, and you will be fired.

12

THE VIEW FROM ABOVE:

Rewards of the Presidential Panorama

It would be fitting to end this dissertation on such a note of finality, since dismissal is the ultimate fate of many college presidents and you must accept this risk before starting up the Ivy Ladder. Fitting, but not fair, because it would rob you of reading about the pleasures of being a college president. If pleasure is not to be the end result of all this painful climbing, it would have been better to stay on the faculty rung and accept tenure, a course of action that would have avoided all the heartburn brought on by administrative duties.

There is little doubt that you will achieve your goal of becoming a college president, providing you have studied and taken advantage of all the lessons that have been taught here. For the sake of discussion, we will assume that the board of trustees of a small but good liberal arts college has heard of your reputation and has selected you to lead it to greatness.

The Best Period of Your Presidency

The best period of your presidency will come the night of your appointment, when you are lying in bed and are not yet asleep. It is during these hours that you are permitted dreams of glory. After long years as one of the mob, you are now head of the mob. Abuses that you have noted, but have been powerless to correct, now will be remedied by your steady hand at the wheel of leadership.

As a qualified and idealistic educator, you no doubt will decide to spend all your waking hours improving the academic abilities of your new college. To do this, you decide to steer a middle course between the old right, which believes that no change is sufficient change, and the new left, which decrees that only students have the maturity and knowledge to reform higher education. Just before rolling over to go to sleep, you resolve that you will start on your program the very next morning.

. . . and the Next Day

Dawn comes, and you wake up and go to work, and discover that the director of development has arranged fat-cat appointments for you for the next month, and you will have time for little else.

The director of development regards you solely as a piece of new merchandise that he must persuade his customers to buy, even though they have grown accustomed to the previous goods. One of your first calls will be on the plumpest cat available. Over dinner and cocktails you discuss your educational philosophy: how you would like to give students a bigger voice in their education, how you would prefer more independent study, and how you would like to make the curriculum more meaningful. You express your opinion that you would rather pour money into academic programs than into shiny new buildings.

The plump cat nods throughout all this and then thanks you for coming.

Afterwards, you ask the director of development, "How did I do?"

"Wonderful," he replies. "That was a unique approach."

Back at the college, the director of development walks into the office of the business manager, sinks into a chair, and moans, "He blew it."

You make much the same pitch to the alumni association, gathered to welcome you to the presidency. The more you talk about changing the college from the way it was when they were students, the less enthusiastic the applause. Afterwards, the president of the alumni association whispers to the director of development, "Is this guy a radical?"

At your first faculty meeting, you tell the professors your ideas about teaching: You request that they try to communicate knowledge to the students by speaking English instead of obscure pedantic double talk. You suggest that they might be doing something wrong if students learn less from listening to them than by reading a book in the library. You also argue that it is not wholly fair to modern students to judge the value of a curriculum by standards that were set up fifty years ago. Afterwards, veteran faculty members call an emergency meeting to discuss ways to circumvent you.

Finally, you address the students. You tell them that you want to open valid lines of communication between the students, faculty and administration. While you don't believe they should run the college, you want their views taken into consideration when professors and administrators make decisions that affect them. At the student union, later, the general agreement is that you are the same old baloney wrapped in a new package.

Maybe You'll Like Ulcers

Perhaps it will dawn on you that a college president, faced with conflicting demands from his constituents, has as much freedom of action as a star attraction in a zoo. If you seek changes, everyone but the students will consider you an innovator; to them you'll be a reactionary no matter what you do. However, if you wish to carry out your dreams of glory by spending more time planning academic programs than in studying building blueprints, feel free to try.

Maybe you are a martyr, who likes ulcers. At least ulcers are preferable to being eaten by lions. The fact that we have progressed to the point where martyrs are no longer thrown to the animals like fodder reflects the educational role of colleges throughout history. You would do well to consider this point. Now we have electric can openers, credit cards, Truth in Packaging, and token integration, all of which represent improvements to the human race due largely to education. Of course there also are wars, open segregation, riots in the streets and on campuses, and other malfunctions of society. These can be laid either to a failure of the home environment or to violence on television, and not to a general inadequacy of the world's educational systems.

If you look at the situation from the standpoint that it is either the fault of parents or Madison Avenue, you can see that the process of reform may not be worth an ulcer, since there is so much to reform that is beyond your control. Failure to take the route of reform also will mean that you can place yourself on the same moral plateau as your colleagues and the alumni association. Most professional academic advisors, particularly the directors of development, will urge that you continue on the safe beaten path that has been trodden by your predecessors. They believe that history has shown that what is good for annual giving is good for society.

Furthermore, status-quoism is cheaper, and some of the money you save by not lowering the teacher/student ratio can be used for other worthwhile purposes, such as landscaping. As for your aims for a better educational system, it is sufficient to write them up in the catalogue. If you keep repeating the sentence, "We provide a first-class education," your constituents will get around to believing it. Should anyone insist on proof, you can cite the number of students who go on to graduate school.

So why not have fun, and enjoy the unique advantages of being a college president?

Some Ego Massage

There is, first of all, the matter of prestige. A college president is high on the scale of status, and you will be treated with the respect due your position wherever you go. Members of the United States Government will assure you that they weigh your words when you speak out on the great issues of the day. Industrial firms will be pleased to consider you as a potential member of their boards. Undoubtedly you will be asked to serve on commissions that will study weighty problems. The presence of a college president on boards of directors and commissions lends credence to the proceedings.

The nice thing is that you won't have to go to any meetings, since only your name and position count, and they are listed on the letterhead.

You will, however, have to attend many graduations to receive honorary degrees and deliver commencement addresses. If there is one thing college presidents have in common, it is their love of giving honorary degrees to colleagues when they can't find a more important speaker.

The job itself does wonders for your ego, and if you have had the initial ambition and drive to aim for a college presidency, you will have an ego that needs constant massaging. The prime masseuse will be your secretary; it is a necessary qualification for the position. She will soothe you when you are troubled, and inflate you with flattery on the one or two days a year that you have self-doubts. If you make what you believe was an incorrect decision, she will tell you, "It wasn't all that bad" or "I'm sure you won't regret it a month from now when you have more perspective."

In the springtime, your secretary will fill your office with freshly cut flowers, symbol of purity and beauty and protection from life's hard knocks.

She also will shield you from unpleasantness, such as a division chairman who wants to complain about his budget allocation. Without your ever knowing it, you will spend many leisure hours "in conference" while Division waits outside until he finally gives up and goes away to teach something.

A good secretary will so isolate you from what she thinks you want to avoid that the college may collapse without your ever knowing it. This is not really to be desired, but the process does save you from having to make unpopular decisions.

Above all, however, your secretary will be good for your peace of mind, and peace of mind should be one of the rewards of ultimate success.

Not only your secretary, but everyone, will work to keep you happy. As president, you are the most powerful force in the life of nearly everyone on campus. To the faculty, you are the one who can approve either tenure or a rise in rank. To the students, you are the one who can write letters of recommendation to prospective employers, or overrule a decision by the faculty judiciary committee that calls for expulsion. To the football coach, you are the one who can decide whether good sportsmanship is of more intrinsic value than a winning record.

No one wants to see you in anything but a good mood.

It may come as a surprise when the whole campus explodes in frustration or anger, but you can tell the board of trustees, "Not one person informed me they were unhappy; it must be the work of outside agitators."

Where Do You Go from Here?

Meanwhile you can start planning for your future. This is a problem, since there is not much demand for former college presidents. Industrial firms wish to have you on their board of directors while you are in office, but they are not keen on having you take over the company once you either become an emeritus or have been fired. You, on the other hand, will find it difficult to work for one of these firms in another capacity, such as salesman.

If you have come this far, it is best to keep looking upward. Foundations might like to have you as a highly paid consultant or as their president, so it is best to seek foundation money yourself rather than give the task to the director of development. Personal contact will not only help you get the funds you want, but your presence may cause a foundation officer to say, "I'd like to have that man with us one day."

Another acceptable move is to go on to become president of a college that is both larger and better than yours. Since every college in the country thinks it is better than most others, you will have many to choose from. One advantage of inviting presidents of other colleges to speak at your commencement exercises is that they might be retiring and will recommend you as their successor. Invite old presidents.

This, of course, will entail many meetings with the trustees of that college, and you must be up on your fund-raising terminology or you will not be in the running. Keep throwing "deferred giving" in their faces.

Finally there is politics. Forgetting military service and the rise of General Eisenhower, consider Senator J. William Fulbright, who went from the presidency of the University of Arkansas eventually to the chairmanship of the Senate Foreign Relations Committee. Of course, there is the most spectacular example of all, Woodrow Wilson; it would be a good idea to read as many biographies of Wilson as you can get the college librarian to buy for you.

You can enter politics in your home state. As a college president, you should have a great deal of exposure, since the governor is certain to ask you and other presidents to serve on commissions. This enables the governor to seem interested in education, a political necessity. It also gives you state-wide exposure. If you don't have state-wide exposure, you are either lacking in ambition or else you need a new director of public relations.

Two schools of thought exist on whether you should get involved in politics on a partisan basis. The first says that you should. Despite the risks of failure, you must work within the party so that you can climb upwards to the nomination.

The other opinion is the opposite. It says that you should stay aloof, maintain your pose as one of the most intelligent and capable men in the state, and see whether it is the Republicans or the Democrats who are the first to ask you to run. You can then start to shape your political principles. Mostly, however, you will be able to campaign on a platform of a bachelor's degree in every pot. No one, Republican or Democrat, will quarrel with your ideals.

Give the Brat His Diploma

Whatever you do, you will look back upon your days as a college president with feelings of satisfaction. No doubt you occasionally will grimace at how you were required to sell good portions of your soul and conscience in order to get a large contribution. The boredom of faculty meetings may leave such a permanent scar that once a month, from 2 to 6 p.m. on Wednesdays, you will involuntarily shudder at the thought of the momentous battles between divisions. While you undoubtedly will encounter and become good friends in later years with your former students, you may weep for some of the others who came to college for a joy ride and the union card of a diploma.

What you will remember most will be the end-of-the-year rituals known as commencements or graduations. Amidst all the pomp and circumstance, you will look out at the professors in their sometimes gaudy and pretentious academic robes and reflect that although they may have fought with themselves and with you, they at least distributed knowledge to the best of their ability. You also will be kind enough to smile on those who had no ability.

What of the students themselves, who look embarrassed, proud and unusually kempt in the traditional caps and gowns that signify both an end and a beginning? One will come marching up to the platform to receive his degree from your hand, and both of you know that during all his years in college he was a troublemaker who fought the president, the dean and the faculty, and ignored all the rules and made his own regulations, because he felt he was right. You will both overlook all that now, since the battles are over and you both, hopefully, were the winners.

You give the diploma to the brat, and you both grin and shake hands, and he walks down the steps, arrogant as ever, and sees his parents, and neither he nor they can fight back the tears of sadness and joy at this milestone in his life.

So it will all have been worth while, and, despite the heartaches and frustrations, you will have accomplished something. Furthermore, you will be able to reflect on the greatest reward there is for a president of a college: once you reach this lofty position, there will be no need for you ever to read a book again, and for the first time in years, you can sit down and enjoy the Sunday comics without a guilty conscience.

POSTSCRIPT

Having come this far, you deserve an incentive bonus:
As this book was being finished, the Carnegie Commission on Higher Education issued a series of recommendations for the future of American colleges and universities. The report, made public in December 1968, called for the creation of 550 new colleges. Each would need a president. The Commission, headed by Clark Kerr, former president of the University of California, has performed a singular service for readers of these pages.

To illustrate further, here is an excerpt from the *Time* magazine account of the Carnegie report:

"The basic recommendation calls for an expanded program of federal 'educational opportunity grants' to 1,000,-000 students who could not otherwise afford college. Under the terms of the proposed grants, direct federal assistance would go to students rather than colleges. As a result, colleges would find themselves competing for students.

The law of the market place would prevail, and institutions would have extra incentive to attract students by making courses more responsive to their needs and desires. Since tuition alone no longer covers the cost of college instruction, additional federal assistance would be funneled directly to the colleges in proportion to the number of extra students."

Since this one paragraph contains a summary of many of the philosophies discussed in these pages, you can see that the future is bright, both for you and for higher education in the United States.

Just think—550 openings for directors of admissions who can compete for students in the market place; 550 opportunities for directors of public relations to write brochures pointing out that their college's courses are "more responsive to student needs and desires" than those of any other college; 550 chances for presidents to emphasize that "tuition alone no longer covers the cost of college instruction." It is an exciting prospect.

Therefore we should collectively thank the Carnegie Commission for its timely and perceptive report, and urge that its recommendations be adopted as quickly as possible. The sooner those 550 colleges are built, the sooner they will be staffed by you and your fellow readers.

DATE DUE